BLUES

THE BASICS

- Gives a brief introduction to this popular musical style
- Covers key artists, from Ma Rainey and Bessie Smith to Charley Patton and Robert Johnson to B.B. King and Robert Cray
- Includes a complete list of key recordings, videos, websites, and books

Blues: The Basics gives a brief introduction to a century of the blues, ideal for students and interested listeners who want to learn more about this important musical style. The book is organized chronologically, focusing on the major eras in blues' growth and development. Each chapter includes a timeline relating significant social and historical events to developments in the blues. The book concludes with lists of key recordings, books, and videos.

Blues: The Basics serves as an excellent introduction to the players, the music, and the styles that make blues an enduring and well-loved musical style.

Dick Weissman is Emeritus Professor of Music and Music Industry Studies at the University of Colorado at Denver. He has published many books on music, including *The Music Business: Career Opportunities and Self-Defense*. He is also a performing guitarist and has recorded as both a solo artist and session musician.

You may also be interested in the following Routledge Student Reference titles:

BLUES: THE BASICS

Dick Weissman

FOLK MUSIC: THE BASICS

Ronald Cohen

JAZZ: THE BASICS

Christopher Meeder

OPERA: THE BASICS

Denise Gallo

WORLD MUSIC: THE BASICS

Richard Nidel

BLUES
THE BASICS

dick weissman

Routledge
Taylor & Francis Group

NEW YORK AND LONDON

Published in 2005 by
Routledge
Taylor & Francis Group
270 Madison Avenue
New York, NY 10016
www.routledge-ny.com

Published in Great Britain by
Routledge
Taylor & Francis Group
2 Park Square
Milton Park, Abingdon
Oxon OX14 4RN
www.routledge.co.uk

10 9 8 7 6 5 4 3 2 1

Library of Congress Cataloguing-in-Publication Data
  Weissman, Dick.
    Blues: the basics / by Dick Weissman.
      p. cm.
    Includes bibliographical references (p.   ).
    ISBN 0-415-97067-9 (hb : alk. paper) — ISBN 0-415-97068-7 (pb : alk. paper)
    1. Blues (Music)—History and criticism.   I. Title.

    ML3521.W45 2004
    781.643'09—dc22   2004019116

CONTENTS

INTRODUCTION

In the early years of the twenty-first century, the blues — which, to the best of our knowledge, date from the 1890s — have grown in popularity and influence from a little-known regional style found among African Americans to a worldwide phenomenon. The blues are the heartbeat of rock and roll, and they are still played, albeit in another form, by the most advanced jazz musicians. Blues artists successfully tour the globe, communicating beyond the limitations of the English language. A CD reissue of an obscure Mississippi bluesman named Robert Johnson has sold over a million copies, and contains fervent tributes written by Eric Clapton and Keith Richards. There are blues museums, magazines, and numerous books devoted to blues singers, movies and documentary films devoted to the blues, and blues societies all over the world.

What is it about the blues that has taken the idiom from its specialized birthplace to worldwide popularity? There is the fascination of the amazing number of intricate guitar styles that have developed, the soulfulness of the singing that seems to communicate beyond the limitations of a specialized vernacular style, and the expressiveness of the lyrics. The audience for the blues has moved far beyond its original enthusiasts, and the vast number of blues recordings and performances indicate an ongoing and increasing fascination with the music.

In this brief work, we will explore the origins and development of the blues, and how they have evolved to their present popularity. But before we move forward, it might be useful to discuss why the blues seem to be relevant today, over 110 years after they first appeared on the scene.

First, it is critical to understand that the blues developed in an environment characterized by extreme privation and social inequality. As we will see, most critics and music historians place this time around 1890. Some claim that it all started in the Mississippi delta, whereas others feel that it was something that was almost an independent and simultaneous invention in various southern African American communities or locales.

In any case, the social milieu that surrounded the blues was one of suffering, privation, and inequality. After the Civil War, the southern United States went through a period known as Reconstruction when Union soldiers occupied the region. During Reconstruction, schools were established for African Americans, churches were built, black men were elected to local, statewide, and even congressional office, and, for the first time, some black farmers were able to purchase land. However, by the mid-1870s, the tide had reverted back to social conditions that were similar to those in place during the slavery era. Blacks were denied the right to vote by poll taxes (a fee charged to the voter before he could cast a ballot) or "grandfather clauses" (laws that stated that a person could not vote unless his grandfather had voted). White landowners instituted the sharecropper system, where black farmers did not own the land, but worked it in return for a percentage of the crops that were harvested. Often this percentage turned out to be so low that it produced little or no actual money, so that the black sharecropper was virtually a slave. Most social historians consider the period from 1890 to 1920 the period of maximum oppression and prejudice directed against African Americans.

In addition, a system of racial segregation came into play that placed blacks in separate schools, separate train cars, the back of buses, and denied them accommodations or food in public places. Illegal and violent tactics shored up these practices. Cross burnings and threats by armed and masked whites organized by such groups as the Ku Klux Klan intimidated blacks from attempting to assert their rights as free citizens. The most ferocious custom of all was lynching, where not only were blacks murdered, but they were strung up on trees as a sort of horrible example to their brothers and sisters of what awaited "troublemakers". Lynching was the punishment accorded to black men who so much as looked at white women as possible sexual partners, besides being almost the obligatory white response to any direct sexual contact between black men and white women. Of course, sexual contact between white males and black women was essentially ignored, if not tolerated, by the white power apparatus. This inequity was underscored by the discovery that J. Strom Thurmond, the recently deceased conservative senator from South Carolina, fathered a black daughter around 1930.

It was during this period of maximum oppression that the blues developed and flowered. The logical question, long after social conditions have changed to the point where once again blacks are being elected to local, statewide, and national offices, when segregation, at least in public places, has long been outlawed, is why would the blues be a relevant social and musical form, and to whom and on what basis does this relevance exist?

In examining the blues repertory, we realize that a wide variety of subjects and musical forms come under the general category of "the blues." Many blues focus on romantic problems between men and women, others are simply exhortations to party and have a good time, and some discuss social and even economic conditions. Others simply discuss cities, railroad trains, magic, or whatever is running through the mind of the singer-composer. But possibly the best way to look at the context of the blues is to see the blues as a music of various complaints — about men, women, social conditions, or anything else — which may account for their continuing appeal. In the world of the twenty-first century, we are surrounded by a marvelous but dehumanizing technology that brings us amazing things, but cannot provide happiness, or an answer to our individual problems. Although many younger African Americans do not relate closely to the blues, because they have not grown up in the same world that their grandparents experienced, many younger whites (or brown or yellow people) see the blues as an expressive tool that can detail their feelings about life in general, or about the nature of their own lives. Others relate to the party or dance aspects of the blues, and do not spend a lot of time thinking about the message of the music.

In any case, with videos, television specials, radio shows, hundreds of CD reissues, and festivals and other performances, 2003 truly was the Year of the Blues.

SOME CAVEATS

Most of our knowledge of American popular music from the end of the nineteenth century until the mid-twentieth century is dependent upon recordings. There were no blues scholars present at the inception of the blues, and many of the first collectors wrote down texts, but not the melodies of the songs. Before 1945, recordings did not utilize tape, so that most of what we are working with, for the first 50 or so years of the blues' history, is necessarily songs that last for about two and a half minutes (the time limit of a 10-in., 78 rpm disc). We know that blues served as dance music in juke joints and at parties, but we really have no idea of the way that they were performed in that environment. Did the artists simply repeat the songs endlessly, or improvise instrumental solos, or make up extra verses? There really is no way for us to know the answers to these questions.

Another interesting question is whether we really know which musicians were the most important and influential ones. Possibly some of the most inventive or creative musicians never got to record. Timothy Duffy is a blues fan who established a nonprofit foundation, called the Music Maker Relief Foundation. Since 1994 he has traveled all over the south looking for old blues musicians, helping them to record and to get playing jobs, and providing assistance to them in the form of money to buy medicine or even musical instruments. In Duffy's book *Music Makers' Portraits and Songs from the Roots of America,* he and his wife, along with several friends, provide biographical sketches of several dozen blues artists. The majority of these usually older artists had not recorded until Duffy found them, and with the exception of a handful, they were mostly entirely unknown. This would indicate that if we were looking for little-known musicians in, say, 1930, we would have been able to find hundreds of them scattered all over the southern United States. Once again, how can we know that the artists who got to record were necessarily the best or most interesting ones?

The reader should keep these questions in mind when reading this or other books. It simply is not possible for us to know exactly how the blues developed, or who the major figures really were.

THE ROOTS OF THE BLUES: 1619–1919

1910	The *Journal of American Folklore* published extensive article by Howard Odum that included numerous blues texts collected in Georgia, 1906–1908
1912	First sheet music publication of blues songs
1914	World War I began
1917	United States entered the war
	First jazz recording by white Original Dixieland Jazz Band
1919	Race riots took place in Chicago, Charleston, S.C., East St. Louis, Houston, and in many other major U.S. cities

This chapter will introduce us to the blues in various ways. First, we will trace the history of the blues, from their African American roots through various nineteenth-century African American musical styles, including worksongs, spirituals, and popular "minstrel" songs. We will then examine the social conditions at the time of the birth of the blues, and how these conditions influenced the new musical form. We will take a look at some early outgrowths from blues, including ragtime and the beginnings of jazz. We will then briefly examine the typical structure of a blues song. Finally, for those interested in playing blues music, we will give some basic pointers about how to learn to perform them.

HISTORY AND ORIGINS OF THE BLUES

Where did the blues come from? When did they start, and where did they first appear? The blues are an African American form, so it is natural to seek the answers to these questions in the history of how Africans came to the United States, and what music they brought with them.

Most Africans came to the United States as slaves. The first slaves were brought here in 1619, and the slave trade lasted until 1809, with the illegal importation of slaves continuing up until the Civil War. It is generally acknowledged that most of the slaves imported into the United States came from West Africa, although many different tribes and languages were represented. Although there are no absolutely reliable estimates of how many slaves were brought in illegally, one estimate puts the number at 54,000. However, the precise number of Africans removed from their homes is a matter of some controversy and conjecture. We know that for every slave who reached the United States many died in the inhuman and overcrowded conditions aboard the slave ships. Some committed suicide, throwing themselves overboard rather than accepting life as slaves.

Some of the ship captains actually compelled the slaves to sing and dance on the slave ships — believing that the exercise from dancing would help keep them healthy during the dangerous trip — and we have reports that some of these songs appeared to be laments about the exile of the slaves. Slaves were not allowed to bring instruments from Africa, so the music on board the ships was entirely vocal music. The slaves were brought up on deck, and although they were kept in chains in order to avoid any form of protest or revolt, they were encouraged to dance. At times, they were even whipped if they did not dance. It is presumed that *some* musical instruments came over with their owners, but we do not know exactly what these instruments were. We do know that the playing of drums, certainly common in virtually every African tribe, was discouraged by the slave owners. There are reports of slaves playing the fiddle or the banjo in various eighteenth-century journals, and paintings that show slaves playing banjos. Cecilia Conway, in her book *African Banjo Echoes in Appalachia,* lists 12 references to black banjoists prior to 1800, and another 21 references printed by 1856. Dena Epstein, in her book *Sinful Tunes and Spirituals: Black Folk Music to the Civil War,* reports references to slaves playing the fiddle as early as the 1690s, and references to slave banjoists date back to 1754 and 1774. She also writes that simple flutes like quills and pipes were used, and that by the eighteenth-century black fiddlers were a normal part of the musical scene on the plantation. Obviously, the slave musicians also entertained their own people when not performing for the whites.

In his book *Savannah Syncopators,* Paul Oliver mentions that Robert Winans examined the slave narratives collected by the Work Progress Administration (WPA) during the 1930s. Winans found 295 references by ex-slaves to fiddle players, 106 to banjo players,

30 to the playing of the quills (or panpipes), and only 8 to drums. There are also numerous references to slaves playing musical instruments in the form of written advertisements seeking the return of escaped slaves, or in flyers where masters were attempting to sell slaves, which listed their musical talents as a sort of bonus to enhance the salability of the slave. Other instruments reported are the bones, the jawbone of an ass scraped with a wire or brush, tambourine, and the thumb piano (*mbira*).

The banjo itself seems to be a descendant of an instrument from Senegal called the *halam*, which like the five-string banjo has one string that runs about three quarters of the way up the neck of the instrument. In both instruments, the highest and lowest strings are adjacent to one another, and the African playing technique of using the fingernails of the right index and middle fingers and the thumb parallel early American banjo styles.

Some slave owners encouraged the slaves to play music, sing, or dance, feeling that it was a harmless diversion that could amuse the master and mistress. A happy slave was less apt to consider rebellion, might tend to work harder, and might have a better feeling about his or her life. On the other hand, the master could not really control the content of the slave's songs. If the songs were sung in any sort of African dialect, dangerous information could be spread. Even without the use of the African language, lyrics could carry coded messages with different meanings for the slave and the plantation owner. A well-known blues song underscores this duality, stating, "when I'm laughing, I'm laughing just to keep from crying."

Dancing might represent an even clearer danger to the master class, because dance is intrinsically sensuous and potentially erotic. The planter class was ambivalent about black eroticism, seeing it as a sort of devilish temptation not only to the slaves but also to their owners. Such eroticism might lead to potentially "immoral" behavior.

As slavery developed, it became increasingly centered in the southern states. For the most part, the north did not have large farms or need a labor force to work these farms. There was also a certain amount of early antislavery sentiment in the north from groups such as the Quakers in Philadelphia, who regarded slavery as evil.

AFRICAN MUSICAL TRAITS IN AFRICAN AMERICAN MUSIC

Various authors have delineated African musical traits that they feel are traceable in the music of black Americans. These traits include:

- *Flatting of the third and seventh notes of the scale, and sometimes the fifth as well.* (In the key of C these notes would be E, B, and G, respectively.)
- *A metronome sense.* Metronome sense is a clear delineation of where the beats of a measure are located.
- *Music is functional, rather than designed to be "beautiful."* Worksongs were used while people were working; other forms of music might be used for dancing, for religious purposes, or for personal expression.
- *Call-and-response singing.* Call-and-response singing occurs when one person sings a part, and multiple voices answer. In his book *Origins of the Popular Style,* Peter Van Der Merwe points out that dialogue can be another form of call and response, as when a guitar answers a vocal phrase in a blues song.
- *Special vocal techniques.* These include *melisma* (the use of several notes in singing a single syllable) and specialized vocal techniques, such as falsetto or growling.
- *Musical instruments.* A number of African musical instruments were played by African Americans. These include the banjo, bones, mouth-bow, quills, tambourine, and diddley bow, a one-string instrument mounted on a board. Many of the early blues guitarists used the diddley bow as their first instrument, often in their childhood.
- *Use of handclapping.* There were numerous reports of the slaves "patting juba," using handclaps as part of a dance or song.

Whatever parallels we find in African music and the blues, we need to keep in mind that we do not have any recorded examples of African music or blues from the late nineteenth century, the time when scholars believe the blues first evolved. We should also note that the savannah — the part of Africa that spawned musical instruments that were similar to the ones slaves played in

America — was an Arabic culture, whose use of vocal shakes and vibrato is found in African American music. Arabic music also featured the lengthening of individual notes, a quality that puzzled some early white (and classically trained black) musicians when they first heard blues singers, because they could not understand the structure of the music. In other words, Africa does not contain a single musical style, or culture, and African influences are more complex than many scholars have acknowledged.

One of the confusing aspects of attempting to trace African elements in African American music is that the importation of slaves was continuous from 1619 until 1807. The slaves came from various tribes and linguistic groups, and there were differences in the music among the various tribal groups. Not only do we have to factor in all of the different tribes and languages that originally came here, but as new groups of slaves appeared, they in turn would be bringing in whatever influences they had been subject to at the time of their capture. These new arrivals interacted with second- and third-generation slaves, who to some extent were already integrated into American musical practices, or had developed their own fusions of African and American music. Since this is a 250-year period, and we know virtually nothing about African music at any point in the process, it is virtually impossible to make any definitive connections between "original" African music and the new African American forms that developed. Given these circumstances, scholarship necessarily turns into speculation.

AFRICAN AMERICAN SPIRITUALS

The first music performed by African Americans that gained recognition on the larger American musical scene was the so-called African American spiritual. Many slave owners encouraged blacks to attend church, and the imagery of freedom from bondage on earth, "escaping" to a promised land, must have resonated with the slaves' own situation of oppression. Plus, singing hymns would have been acceptable to the white masters, whereas secular songs and dances might have been seen as more threatening.

The first black minister given a license to preach was George Leile Kiokee, who set up an African Baptist Church in Savannah in 1780. In 1801, a free black man named Richard Allen published the first hymnbook for blacks, and established his own church. Allen used quite a few of the Isaac Watts hymns, and he also added lines and phrases to existing white hymns.

The first example of the music of black Americans in print appeared in 1867 in the book *Slave Songs of the United States.* Almost all the songs are hymns or religious songs, with a small representation of secular songs; so it reinforced the notion that African American music centered on the spiritual. The authors refer to improvisation of texts, and "shouting," or dramatic emotive singing taking place in a circle or ring. This book's 102 songs were collected from 1861 to 1864 primarily by the book's authors — William Francis Allen, Charles Pickard Ware, and Lucy McKim Garrison — who were working in an educational program on the Port Royal Islands, off the coast of South Carolina. Allen, Ware, and Garrison found no musical instruments among the singers they knew, and remark that it was difficult to get freedmen to sing the older songs, attributing this fact to the ex-slaves repudiating the "undignified" aspects of their past lives.

Black religious songs were referred to as "Negro spirituals." Spirituals were songs with religious themes, often looking toward a better life in heaven after the singer's time on earth was over. However, the songs also sometimes contained double meanings, known as *coded messages*. The songs could have one meaning to the singers and a black audience, and an entirely different one to any white listeners. The messages could involve analogies between biblical oppression and the plight of the slaves, or could even offer directions for help in escaping from the plantation, as in the song *Follow the Drinking Gourd.*

Spirituals are generally regarded as folk songs that evolved through the process of oral transmission — songs that were passed on from one person to another and then changed either deliberately or accidentally. The spirituals were sung by groups of people, rather than individuals, and generally utilized the call-and-response pattern in which a singer would sing a line or a verse, and then the group would chime in with a response to that line, or would wait until the chorus of the song.

The first successful "serious" African American performing group was the Fisk Jubilee Singers, who performed highly arranged versions of spirituals in harmonized settings. Formed in the 1870s at Fisk University in Nashville to raise money for the all-black college, the group toured in the United States and eventually Europe, and made some early recordings of their "concert" versions of spirituals. They influenced countless other groups, and again helped solidify the notion that the spiritual was the "highest" form of African American music. Twenty-five of their songs were published in souvenir programs that were sold when the group performed, and in 1872, an entire volume of their repertoire appeared. This book went through many editions, and was very influential in spreading spirituals to a broader audience.

The Fisk singers were so successful in their fund-raising efforts that a number of other schools, such as the Hampton Institute and Tuskegee Choir, attempted similar touring and fund-raising efforts. Other groups not connected with schools also began to compete with the Fisk groups, including some bogus groups that attempted to use the "Jubilee Singers" name without permission. The performances by these groups leaned toward formal arrangements, often with piano accompaniment.

The history of the spiritual, then, involves European sources — early hymnbooks — that were reworked by African American musicians to form a new musical style. This interplay between black and white is typical of much of the history of American popular music. Nonetheless, throughout the twentieth century, there was an extended controversy as to whether white hymns came from black spirituals, or vice versa. The proponents for the white origins of spirituals were in effect arguing that African Americans lacked the superior inventiveness of their white compatriots. Black scholars took the opposite view, presenting a view of slaves as relentlessly creative human beings, endowed with more musical talent than their white contemporaries.

George Pullen Jackson, the foremost advocate for the white origin of spirituals, related the tunes of several hundred African American spirituals to tunes found in the British Isles. He also found parallels in the use of the flatted third and seventh notes of the scale that are usually attributed to African Americans. However, Jackson did not spend much time analyzing the texts, nor did he factor in the improvisational aspects of musical performances. Melodies in folk tradition are not stagnant, but change from one performance to another. Not surprisingly some black scholars claimed earlier origins of the black songs. These scholars pointed out that the first publication of the songs did not necessarily prove an earlier origin than songs that might have been sung without ever having been published. The truth probably lies somewhere in between. Dena Epstein sees the development of spirituals as an exchange of songs during the early-nineteenth-century camp meetings that both whites and blacks attended.

A number of black composer-arrangers, such as John W. Work, J. Rosamond Johnson, his brother James Weldon Johnson, and Nathaniel Dett, expanded on the work of the Jubilee Singers, and made formal musical arrangements of traditional spirituals. During the twentieth century virtually all black concert or opera singers performed spirituals. Some of the famous performers were Roland Hayes, Paul Robeson, and Marian Anderson.

When the Czech composer Antonin Dvorák visited the United States in 1893, he enthusiastically endorsed the work of the Jubilee Singers, and wrote a symphony, known as *The New World Symphony*, that incorporated melodies that were obviously derived from the spirituals. This work became influential and popular, spreading the influence of the spirituals in yet another arena.

Blues and spirituals share some common musical features, particularly the use of the blues scale. However, there are some fundamental differences between them. One is that spirituals usually referred to a better land awaiting the singers after death, while blues focused on the singer's more immediate or practical needs, especially romantic ones. The blues also gloried in using bawdy images and double entendres, which were not acceptable in spirituals. To put it in another way, the blues were about the here and now, the spirituals were about the afterlife. Blues are generally performed by vocal soloists, whereas the spirituals almost always involved groups of singers.

The two musical forms came together by the 1920s in the form of *holy blues* — songs that utilized blues instruments and musical style, but had religious texts.

EARLY BLACK SECULAR MUSIC

Various travelers, historians, and journalists of the eighteenth and nineteenth centuries make reference to the singing or playing of slaves. In addition to spirituals, they note several different forms of secular songs, including work songs, hollers, and ring shouts. Unfortunately, it was not until the late 1890s that folklorists started to collect folk music in the United States, and it was not until the 1920s that we had recordings of this music. This was also the period when blues, ragtime, and jazz were all developing. Consequently, it is difficult for us to know what the hollers sounded like in their "pure" state, when they were relatively uninfluenced by other musical styles.

One primary difference between the work songs, hollers, and ring shouts and later musical styles was that these songs were sung without any accompanying instruments. It is a safe assumption that more African traits can be found in unaccompanied music. We do have a number of recorded examples of work songs, and some of hollers, but they date from a much later time, and the work songs were mostly recorded in prisons. Writing in 1925, Dorothy Scarborough pointed out that work songs were sometimes performed by a group of people working together, but also might be sung by individuals in cases where slaves were working as a group, but separated from one another.

THE MINSTREL SHOW

Beginning in the early nineteenth century, black secular music came to the attention of many Americans through the vehicle of the *minstrel show*. Scholars date the earliest example of white performers using blackface to the late 1820s. By that time a half-dozen performers toured the nation, performing songs and dances between the acts of plays. Two of the most famous of these performers were Thomas Dartmouth "Daddy" Rice and George Washington Dixon. Author Robert C. Toll, in his book *Blacking Up: The Minstrel Show in Nineteenth-Century America*, reports two of the tunes performed as *Zip Coon* (later known as *Turkey in the Straw*) and *Jump Jim Crow*. The two stereotypical characters of the minstrel show are represented in these two songs: Zip Coon was the well dressed city dweller who knew all the latest trends; Jim Crow was his rural brother, the country bumpkin who stayed home on the farm. In addition to dressing up as plantation black men by using burnt cork on their faces, white performers also sang in African American dialects. Some of the songs of the minstrels, such as "*The Boatman's Dance*, passed into folk tradition, and were still being performed 100 years later.

Complete minstrel shows began during the 1830s, and featured skits, dances, and singing. They were, in effect, mini-theatrical performances that presented blackface comedy and song. There were actors, singers, and instrumentalists, especially banjo and fiddle players. Often the shows made fun of African American's use of language, by presenting it as either pompous or foolish. The show's master of ceremonies was known as The Interlocutor, and typically Tambo and Bones, two comic characters named for the musical instruments that they played — the tambourine and bones — made fun of him. Although slaves were generally portrayed as lazy, shiftless, fun-loving, and irresponsible, occasional minstrel productions depicted them in more human terms.

The first popular minstrel troupe was the Virginia Minstrels, formed in New York City in 1843 by four individuals who had achieved some fame as solo blackface performers: Billy Whitlock, Dan Emmett, Frank Brower, and Dick Pelham. E.P. Christy and his Christy Minstrels were among the most successful of the rapidly developing competitors of the Virginians. The music of these performers had a strong Irish-English tinge, blended with African American styles that many of the artists had heard from performers in the south, and sought to imitate. The banjoists often consciously imitated the work of black musicians, who themselves had been influenced by white dance music, as well as their own musical traditions. The later performing groups were larger, and often featured multiple musicians, two fiddlers and two banjoists, for example, instead of one. One of the most important composers who worked in the minstrel idiom, although not exclusively so, was Stephen Collins Foster, who wrote a number of songs that are still heard today, including *Oh! Susannah* and *Old Folks At Home* (popularly known as *Swanee River*). Foster was not a performer, but is often regarded as America's first professional songwriter; one of his first and best customers was E.P. Christy, who took author credit for some of Foster's first hits. Most of Foster's songs were highly sentimental, and depicted the slave as yearning for his master and the old plantation.

Minstrel songs varied in their attitudes toward slavery. In addition to depicting "the old plantation," some of the songs protested, or at least mentioned, that slavery often led to the break-up of families, as the master sold off a husband without a wife, or vice versa. Several scholars have pointed out that the very fact that there was so much interest in African Americans music and lifestyles was a step forward in the ultimate acceptance of African Americans into American life.

Minstrel shows were popular both in the cities and in the rural areas. Some of the companies had runs as long as 10 years in such cities as Boston, New York, and Philadelphia. However, in the early days of the minstrel show, black performers were rare. William Henry Lane, known as "Master Juba," was one of the few black performers in the early minstrel days. He was considered a magnificent dancer, and was victorious over John Diamond, his white rival, in dancing contests. By the end of the Civil War, many of the touring companies were black, although they were usually owned by white entrepreneurs. A number of jazz performers got their start playing in touring minstrel shows, including W.C. Handy, Ma Rainey, and Bessie Smith. Black minstrel groups drew black audiences, as well as the usual white curiosity-seekers.

By the turn of the twentieth century, minstrel shows were no longer popular in the northern cities, and were replaced by vaudeville shows. Performers such as Al Jolson and Eddie Cantor continued to perform in blackface, however, through the 1920s. The burnt cork tradition continued in rural communities up until World War II.

Early folklorists assumed that the negative imaging of the minstrel shows contributed to the abandonment of the banjo by black musicians. This seemed to be borne out by the fact that, prior to the mid-1970s, the Library of Congress collection of thousands of recorded songs and instrumental pieces included less than a dozen recordings of black old-time banjo players. However, extensive field research by Bruce Bastin, Cecilia Conway, and Tommy Thompson in the mid-1970s turned up far more black musicians who played the five-string banjo. Their picking styles were somewhat similar to those of white players in the Southern Appalachian mountains. This has raised some intriguing but unanswered questions about the relationship between white and black music, and who originated what styles.

THE EARLY BLUES

SOCIAL CONDITIONS AT THE BIRTH OF
THE BLUES: 1870s–1900

After the Civil War, social conditions in the south appeared to change radically for the freedmen. The period 1865–1880 represented a period of hope for southern blacks. There was a general optimism among African Americans, who felt that they were "free at last, free at last." Slavery was abolished, some ex-slaves were able to buy land, and they voted in local and national elections. African Americans were elected to state offices and to the U.S. House of Representatives, and there were even a few elected to the U.S. Senate. Northern troops occupied the south, and missionaries established schools.

However, northern troops withdrew from the south in 1877, and conditions quickly deteriorated. Freedoms were curtailed, and many blacks were barred from voting — either outright or through the imposition of restrictive "poll taxes" or fees charged to exercise the right to vote. The sharecropping system, in which whites owned the land and black workers were forced to pay rent for its use, became common. The blacks also often had to purchase seed and other supplies from the landowners, often at inflated prices, so that most — if not all — of their harvest went to repaying loans and rent. The system was in effect similar to slavery, and some of the sharecroppers were perpetually in debt to the landowners. To aggravate matters, the northerners largely lost interest in the freedmen, and various political deals were made that removed any federal control over the racist practices prevalent in the south.

It is possible to make the case that it was the very nature and extent of repression that led to the dynamic emergence of new musical forms. In *Bleaching Our Roots: Race and Culture in American Popular Music*, performer-scholar Dave Lippman makes the interesting point that the slave owners, attempts to repress African music necessarily led to the development of new and unique musical forms by the slaves. We can hypothesize that the repressive period of 1890–1920 similarly led southern African Americans to create new musical forms.

Unfortunately, we do not have much in the way of printed texts to show us how and when the blues evolved. No one was very interested in secular black music in the late nineteenth century, and of course there were no tape recorders available. What blues scholars have written about really stems largely from the recordings and recollections of the older generation of black blues artists, none of whom recorded before 1920.

However, there is one key source for studying the early blues. Howard Odum collected music in Georgia and Mississippi in 1905–1908 and published his work, initially in *The Journal of American Folklore*, and some 20 years later in two books of songs, coauthored by Guy Johnson. Odum published the first blues, and much of what we have said about the form of early blues comes from his researches. Unfortunately, his books do not specify which songs were collected in which states. Alan Lomax calls Mississippi "the land where the blues began," but we have no absolute evidence that this is literally true. We do know that the ways in which the blues developed vary in different regions, as we will see in Chapter 2.

Odum classifies early blues musicians into three categories:

- The *songster* was a musician who performed blues, but also had a repertoire of many other songs, such as spirituals, work songs, and ballads.
- The *musicianer* was an instrumentalist.
- The *music physicianer* was a musician who traveled, and wrote and played his own songs.

It is possible that the songsters were the bridge between earlier black music forms and the blues. When one remembers that such musicians played for both black and white audiences, and would be attempting to please both groups, this seems even more plausible. The traveling music physicianers would then serve to spread the music far and wide, at least to the black populations in various parts of the country. The distinction between these various musicians has been overdrawn, in the sense that many musicians performed blues, other secular songs, and even religious tunes, and some musicians, such as Lonnie Johnson, sometimes recorded as vocalists, sometimes as an instrumental soloists, and sometimes as accompanists for other vocalists.

Another key early source for our knowledge of the blues comes from musician-composer W.C. Handy. In his autobiography (published many years later), Handy recalls seeing a black musician sitting by a railroad station in 1903, playing guitar with a knife in his left hand and singing *I'm goin' where the Southern cross the Yellow Dog*. Handy found that this song referred to a railroad junction in Morehead, Mississippi. There are other reports of the blues sung during the 1890s in the memoirs of various black musicians. Some blues singers have claimed that the song *Joe Turner* was the first blues song, and the others that developed were variations on it. Turner was a penal officer who transported convicts in Tennessee between 1892 and 1896, certainly the correct time period for the beginnings of the blues.

Handy was a trained musician who realized that the blues could bring him income and popularity. Not long after his first experience of hearing the blues, Handy's band was playing a dance in Cleveland, Mississippi, and saw a guitar, mandolin, and string bass trio play during the intermission of their show. The audience rewarded the trio's efforts with "a rain of silver dollars," causing Handy to immediately realize the financial potential of the folk blues. Because Handy was a bandleader, he needed to formalize the structure of the blues, and to write the blues down in sheet music form. Handy's *Memphis Blues* was published in in 1912, and his *St. Louis Blues* appeared in 1914. Handy used the AAB lyric form, and his songs were usually 12-bar blues (we will discuss the structure of a blues song shortly). The first blues vocal to be recorded was Handy's *Memphis Blues*, but, ironically, it was recorded by white musician Morton Harvey.

Handy's success inspired countless others to write "blues" songs, and this repertoire became known in the 1910s and 1920s as the "classic blues." Unlike their folk forebears, classic blues were composed blues songs, generally with a definite musical structure and a story line, and they were sung by female singers, many of whom were experienced performers, used to singing in front of theater audiences. This was very different from the style of folk blues, which were performed before small, informal audiences, or at dances. We will discuss the development of classic blues in Chapter 2.

SUBJECT MATTER

The blues that Howard Odum found in Georgia and Mississippi before 1910, like the blues that are sung today, were largely about romantic situations between men and women. Some of the songs contained boastful lyrics about the sexual prowess of the singer, some were self-pitying lyrics about unfaithful women, or double-dealing friends. Some are simply celebrations of sexuality, others of the virtues or difficulties associated with drinking. Another common subject was travel, and often the railroad was mentioned either as a way to escape the often oppressive small-town life, or simply to enjoy a change of scenery. Many blues refer to specific towns or states of the singer's acquaintance. In an unfriendly world, jail was inevitably a possibility, and jail, judges, and prison guards make their way into early blues lyrics. Odum acknowledged that he was unable to print some blues lyrics on the basis of their immorality, the use of "unacceptable" sexual references. The same held true of some later collectors. Consequently, we will never know how many bawdy songs simply never appeared in print.

Various scholars have argued that the blues are a form of protest music, with the singer complaining about his lot in life. Others deny that protest is a significant aspect of blues style. Even in Odum's work we find complaints about jailers, bosses, and work. It is also important to remember that all of the early collectors were white. Many of the singers may have not trusted these scholars enough to sing songs that complained about their lives, or protested specific occurrences. We will return to this subject when we discuss Lawrence Gellert's collections of protest songs from the 1920s and 1930s.

Sometimes early blues lyrics did not tell a single coherent story, but rather used a number of unconnected images of what was floating through the singer's mind at the time of the performance. Sometimes this included combining verses from other songs, and transforming them into "new" creations. There were certainly a number of well-known blues verses that surfaced in various songs. After blues started to appear on records during the 1920s, the pirating of verses from various songs became a common procedure. Sometimes entire songs were "borrowed," with only the most minor changes, such as the singer changing the caliber of a gun or the name of the female protagonist in a song. This is partially due to the fact that record executives demanded that singers "write" their own material, hoping to benefit from ownership of their copyrights; many singers were not talented writers, and so took to reworking older songs in an attempt to pass them off as their own.

Although the slow blues definitely had a plaintive quality, faster tempo blues made good dance or party music. At times a sad lyric was combined with an up-tempo melody, or a faster tempo could mask the feelings of sadness in a thoughtful lyric. The blues had room for a wide range of emotions.

RAGTIME AND EARLY JAZZ

The beginnings of ragtime and jazz virtually paralleled the development of the blues form. In ragtime, unlike the blues, the piano was the main instrument. The early ragtime pianists were barroom players, who did not necessarily read music. Ingredients of ragtime began to appear in the pop songs of the 1890s. Known as "coon songs," these songs enjoyed enormous success and, as one might expect, treated African Americans in a derogatory fashion. They were essentially a repetition of the images that minstrels had painted of African Americans. Ironically, some of the composers of these songs were themselves black.

Instrumental ragtime developed during the 1890s, primarily in St. Louis and Sedalia, Missouri, but also in New Orleans. Eileen Southern, in her pioneering book *The Music of Black Americans*, also mentions piano players in such cities as Mobile, Alabama, Louisville, Kentucky, Memphis, Chicago, Philadelphia, and New York. As instrumental ragtime developed, it became very complex, containing as many as four different musical parts to a song. Composer-performers such as Scott Joplin or James Scott were sophisticated, trained musicians, who thought of themselves as serious composers. The first recorded ragtime pieces appeared in 1912 in two piano rolls recorded by the legendary black piano virtuoso Blind Boone; Joplin made some rolls well after his playing career was over 3 years later.

Ragtime piano was a sophisticated musical style, with the right hand playing syncopated or offbeat figures while the left hand kept the rhythm steady. Not only were such pieces as Joplin's work divided into different sections, there were often key changes from one section to the next. Gilbert Chase, in his book *America's Music*, suggests that the right-hand piano syncopations were derived from black banjo styles played on the five-string banjo. In these styles of banjo playing, the thumb played the fifth string of the banjo, sometimes playing that string off the beat.

Although ragtime was sometimes played on the banjo, the primary impact of ragtime on the blues was in the Piedmont guitar styles of the Carolinas and Georgia. As we will see in the next two chapters, these styles required a more sophisticated harmonic approach to the guitar than that of the folk blues players. The most advanced players, such as Blind Blake, wrote guitar instrumentals, rather than just using the guitar to accompany songs.

Most scholars agree that New Orleans was the central place where jazz developed, although there were black brass bands in various parts of the country in the middle of the nineteenth century. New Orleans had a particularly rich tradition of brass bands, dating from the 1870s. Sometime toward the end of the century, these musicians started to modify ragtime, and "swing the beat." The legendary cornetist Buddy Bolden was probably among the first of these early jazzmen. By the turn of the century such African American musicians as trumpet players Freddie Keppard and Bunk Johnson started to play downtown with the Creole musicians, and New Orleans jazz was born. However, by 1915, many African Americans moved out of the south, and in 1917, the U.S. Navy closed down the Storyville district. Storyville had been the entertainment center of New Orleans, complete with bordellos that employed many musicians. The next developments in jazz took place in Chicago.

Jazz utilized some of the harmonic devices of ragtime, but kept the spirit of the blues. The brass instruments moaned, growled, and bent notes to simulate blues growls and trills. The typical New Orleans combos had trumpet, trombone, and clarinet, and the rhythm section had a tuba instead of a string bass, a banjo, and a small drum set. In a good number of early jazz arrangements, the music was not written down, but was improvised, with beginnings and endings of songs worked out. The solos were entirely improvised.

Many of the early jazzmen played on records by the classic blues singers in the 1920s, although usually with small combos using only a handful of musicians. Oddly the first jazz recordings were made by a white group, The Original Dixieland Jazz Band, in 1917.

BLUES STRUCTURE

When we discussed W.C. Handy and his composition, we mentioned the lyric structure (AAB) and the form "12-bar blues." Students of the blues are familiar with these terms, but for others they may be slightly mystifying. Here is a brief explanation.

If we look at the way blues are performed by a contemporary artist, such as B.B. King, it is easy enough to analyze the musical and lyrical structure of one of his songs. Almost invariably the songs will be in 4/4 time, which means that there are four quarter notes in each measure of music. The verses will contain twelve bars of music, and the chord structure will usually consist of three basic chords, built on the first, fourth, and fifth notes of the scale. In the key of C, these chords will be C, F, and G7, with the C going to a C7 and the F chord moving to an F7. The lyrics will be in AAB form, which means that the first line of the song will be repeated, with the third line acting as a sort of answer to the previous (repeated) lines. The end of lines one and two typically rhymes with the end of line 3. An example, with the chords written in, is:

```
C                                        C7
It's Monday morning, and I don't want to work no more,
F                      F7           C   C7
Yeah it's Monday morning, ain't gonna work no more,
G7                     F            C  F C   G7
Wish I was in Texas, with the sun shining on my door.
```

Notice that there is a short chord sequence at the end of the verse. This is called a *turnaround*, and it leads back to the next verse, which will start with the C chord.

This is all very well, except that when we start to look at the origins of the blues, and how they developed, we find a number of disconcerting things. First, the earlier folk blues did not always contain twelve bars. They might have eleven, or thirteen, sixteen, or even twelve-and-a-half bars. It is quite possible that the twelve-bar form developed when musicians started to play together, or when a singer was accompanied by a guitarist or pianist. As soon as two or more musicians play together, they need to have some agreement about the length of musical phrases in order to stay together. Or perhaps Handy, being a "professional" musician, simply "evened out" a form that in the folk tradition was much more flexible. Blues did not always use three chords, either. Some of the Mississippi blues really consisted of a single chord, slightly modified to go with the melody of a particular song.

The lyrics were equally irregular. Howard Odum, working in 1906–1908, found that there were songs that consisted of a single repeated line, with no additional lyrics. Other lyrics patterns consist of a verse that has an opening line, with the second line repeated, instead of the first line as shown in the example above. This form can be indicated as an ABB form. An example is:

> Ain't no more cotton, cause the boll weevil ate it all,
> Gonna leave this town, goin' away before the fall,
> You know baby, I won't be here next fall.

Notice that in both lyrics the repeated lines are not identical. They are almost conversational, as though the singer is thinking about the lyrics as he sings.

The forms that blues songs can take are seemingly endless, and sometimes vary within a single song. I have an out-of-print recording by Hally Wood where she sings a song called *The Worried Blues*. The first verse goes like this:

> I've got the worried blues,
> I've got the worried blues,
> I've got the worried blues, oh my Lord;
> I've got the worried blues,
> I'm going where I've never been before.

I suppose we could call this form AAAAB. But, later in the song she sings

> I'm going where those orange blossoms bloom,
> I'm going where I never been before,
> I'm going where those orange blossoms bloom, oh my Lord;
> I'm going where those orange blossoms bloom,
> I'm going where I've never been before.

We might call this form ABAAB. The point is that the blues singer created the form around the lyrics of the song, rather than tailoring the lyrics of the song to fit a preconceived model.

At the turn of the twentieth century, there were ballads that had many elements of blues songs, but did not follow these lyric structures. For example, in the song *Frankie and Albert* — a version of the song *Frankie and Johnny* sung by Mississippi John Hurt and Leadbelly, among others — there is a recurrent last line ("he was her man, he was doin' her wrong"). In Furry Lewis's version of the ballad *Casey Jones* — which he calls *Kassie Jones* — he repeats the last (fourth line) of each verse. This form of song, with a repeated last line, is known as a "refrain," and is common in Anglo-American balladry as well.

Just as the blues make use of repetition in the construction of their lyrics, the same patterns also can be found in spirituals, and in traditional English ballads. For example, here is a verse of the sixteenth-century ballad *Pretty Polly*, a song that has been collected in numerous versions in the southern Appalachian mountains:

> I courted pretty Polly, all the livelong night,
> I courted pretty Polly, all the livelong night,
> I left her next morning, before it was light.

The spiritual *Lonesome Valley* has been collected from both white and black singers. It uses a different pattern of repeated phrases:

> You've got to walk that lonesome valley,
> You've got to walk it by yourself,
> Ain't nobody here, going to walk it for you,
> You've got to walk that lonesome valley by yourself.

In this instance, the lyric is not a word-for-word repetition. The second line is slightly different from the first line, and the fourth line combines elements from the first and second lines.

LEARNING TO PLAY OR SING THE BLUES

Before we proceed with the history of the blues, it might be useful for the interested reader to get a glimpse of how to learn to play or sing the blues. The earliest blues singers developed their knowledge of the music as a sort of communal experience, in the same way that communities in such diverse places as Bulgaria and West Africa have nurtured and developed their musical traditions. The Carolinas nurtured and developed the Piedmont blues, while in Texas and Mississippi relevant but different musical styles emerged. Further refinements that scholars ponder over include the differences between the delta Mississippi blues style that developed in the Clarksdale area, and the somewhat different and less intense Mississippi school that emerged around Bentonia, north of the city of Jackson.

One hundred and ten years later these local communities where music could be learned directly from older master performers no longer really exist. So how does the reader, black, white, or otherwise, learn how to play or sing the blues? The most typical path that people follow is to immerse themselves in the musical style through listening to CDs, watching videos, and buying instructional books and tapes. Fortunately, these resources are readily available in most cities, and if you do not live in a relatively large urban area they are available through mail order or internet purchases. In the appendix of this book is a large list of resources that can help. But let us discuss the way that these resources can be utilized most efficiently.

From the author's point of view, the most useful way to learn about a musical style, blues or otherwise, is to have as much direct contact as possible with a person or people for whom that style is natural. In other words, your best bet is to be around blues singers, players, and bands. The reason that this sort of immersion is the most successful way of learning about the blues is that not only will it show you the specific musical ways that, for example, a guitar is played, but it will also give you some feeling for the more subtle aspects of the music. In addition, you will begin to develop enough of an ear to understand what distinguishes one particular player from another. Mance Lipscomb and John Hurt had a similar feel in their playing, but they do not sound alike. Muddy Waters developed out of the Clarksdale tradition that spawned Robert Johnson, Son House, and Charley Patton, but Muddy really did not sound anything like these other blues artists. Each had certain distinguishing traits, whether right-hand picking styles, the use of musical dynamics or different guitar tunings, or vocal styles that could involve falsetto (a sort of fake high tenor) singing, grunts, doubling what the guitar was playing, and so on.

It is more convenient to learn from instructional videos, CDs, and books than to seek out artists who actually play and sing the blues. The problem with learning from these valuable resources is that they are tools, not substitutes for trial-and-error musical experiences. The same thing applies to taking guitar, piano, or vocal lessons. Blues is an improvisational genre of music, and although students often must go through a process of imitating a specific musician, this ultimately can be counterproductive to developing individual approaches to the music. So, the author recommends singing and playing along with records only up to a point. There should come a time when you put other people's styles away, and you make the choice to try it your own way.

Whether or not you will turn out to be a musical innovator is impossible to predict, but there is a great deal of joy to be experienced in playing your own songs, your own instrumental solos, or even your own musical arrangements of old standards.

Summary
The blues began around 1890, possibly in Mississippi. The musical aspects of the blues utilized a number of African traits, and lyrics of the early blues were written in a stream-of-consciousness manner. Rather than telling a specific story, they reflected the moods and memories of the singer. The earliest blues were probably unaccompanied, but the instrument of choice quickly became the guitar. Blues drew on a variety of black popular styles, including spirituals, hollers, and worksongs, and European elements borrowed from ballads, dance tunes, and religious songs. Trained black musicians began to formalize the structure of the blues after 1910, and many of their more structured and pop-oriented songs were sung by women professional performers. Jazz and ragtime developed in a parallel stream to the blues, and these musical styles influenced one another.

THE 1920s: DOCUMENTED BEGINNINGS OF THE CLASSIC AND RURAL BLUES

2

TIMELINE: THE 1920s

1919   The 18th Amendment was enacted, prohibiting the sale and consumption of alcohol. Illegal bars and clubs quickly arose, which often employed musicians, dancers, and other performers.

1920   Mamie Smith recorded for Okeh, and *Crazy Blues* became the first hit blues record.

1923   First Bessie Smith record issued.
        Ralph Peer made the first of his "field" recordings, on location outside the studio, in Atlanta, Georgia.
        Hitler formed the National Socialist Party in Germany.

1924   First recordings of Ma Rainey and of male blues singers Papa Charlie Jackson and Ed Andrews issued.

1925   First recording of Blind Lemon Jefferson. He became the dominant blues artist of the late 1920s. Electrical recording (using microphones) introduced.

1927   Talking movies introduced, leading to the beginning of the end for the black touring theater business.

1929   Great Depression began. Sales of records and record players began to plummet.

We have dated the origins of the blues to the late nineteenth century, and early reports indicate that the blues was a folk-form that originated in the rural areas of the south. Whether it be touring singer Ma Rainey hearing a blues-like lament in 1902 or W.C. Handy watching a roustabout playing guitar with a knife in 1903, the early blues must have been performed by nonprofessional musicians in an informal setting. Unfortunately, we have no recorded examples that preserve these early forms of the music although there are scattered recordings of black strings bands, and even a few performances that indicate blues influences. Among these are a 1904 harmonica solo by Pete Hampton called *Dat Mouth Organ Coon,* and a 1916 record called *Nigger Blues,* by George O'Connor.

Numerous scholars have pointed out that the record companies did not feel that there was a market for blues music, or for that matter much other African American music. There were some recordings of blues in the teens and early 1920s made by white singers, such as vaudeville performers Nora Bayes and Marie Cahill. But it took Perry Bradford — African American composer of popular and blues-styled songs — to convince a recording company, Okeh Records, to record a black singer, Mamie Smith, in February 1920. Ironically, the first songs that Smith recorded were originally going to be cut by white vaudevillian Sophie Tucker. Smith's recording of Bradford's songs *That Thing Called Love* and *You Can't Keep a Good Man Down* was released in July 1920. Okeh did not promote the record, but unexpectedly high sales subsequently brought Smith back to the studio in August, when she recorded her hit song, *Crazy Blues,* backed by *It's Right Here for You (If You Don't Get It/'Tain't No Fault of Mine).* Okeh did considerable advertising for this recording, and their efforts were followed by startling sales. Suddenly record companies began to recognize that there was indeed a market for blues records. Other record companies quickly jumped on the blues bandwagon, with Emerson, Pathé-Frères, and Gennett all quickly issuing blues by female artists. During 1921 and 1922, Godrich and Dixon (in their excellent book, *Recording the Blues*) report that on average around one blues record a week was issued.

The early recorded blues singers were generally cabaret singers, professional performers whose backgrounds were far removed from the original folk blues artists. They did not write their own songs, but relied on songwriters and entrepreneurs such as Clarence Williams and Perry Bradford to provide them with material. The singers were professional performers, so that their diction and phrasing owed more to theatrical training than to the folk variety of blues. The songwriters were professional African American musicians who understood popular music structure and its conventions. The recordings generally utilized small jazz combos for their accompaniment. Instruments such as cornets, clarinets, and banjos are frequently found on these recordings, and many of the players were well-known jazz musicians, such as Louis Armstrong or Fletcher Henderson. A corps of songwriter-musicians, such as Williams, Bradford and female pianist-composer Lovie Austin, functioned as informal bandleaders. Occasionally, the earthier singers, such as Ma Rainey, would use jug bands or guitarists as accompanists to try to capture the rural beginnings of the blues.

There were a great number of women who got to record blues during the 1920s, but a dozen or so artists were the ones who made multiple recordings, toured widely, and enjoyed large sales of their recordings. These so-called classic blues singers included the two dominant figures Ma Rainey and Bessie Smith, and several talented second-tier performers, including Lucille Bogan, Ida Cox, Alberta Hunter, Victoria Spivey, and Sippie Wallace. Among these performers, many wrote their own material. Ma Rainey wrote a large percentage of her own songs, and Cox, Hunter, and Spivey were renowned as writers. Bessie Smith wrote about a sixth of her own songs, while some of the other performers wrote no songs at all. It is difficult to know, 80 years later, how much of a voice the singers had in the selection of their songs, and what level of belief or emotion they were able to bring to material that was chosen for them. Later in this chapter we analyze the differences in subject matter between the songs written by the artists themselves, as opposed to those composed by others.

MA RAINEY AND HER INFLUENCE ON THE BLUES

Bessie Smith recorded several years before Gertrude "Ma" Rainey (1886–1939) had that opportunity, but Ma was actually 8 years older than Bessie, and in fact had served as a bit of a mentor for the younger singer. Ma and her husband "Pa" Rainey billed themselves as "assassinators of the blues." Ma had been touring for some twenty years before she had the opportunity to record. She worked primarily in the south at theaters run by the TOBA, the Theater Owner Booking Association, a consortium of venues catering to black audiences, known less fondly as "Tough On Black Asses" by the many performers who worked these venues. Between 1923 and 1928, Rainey recorded 92 songs for Paramount Records. Of all the women who recorded extensively during the 1920s, Rainey's work was, as her biographer Sandra Leib points out, the least influenced by commercial factors, and the closest to the folk blues tradition.

Rainey performed with numerous touring companies, but her most famous work was with the Rabbit Foot Minstrels. This company was based in Mississippi, and besides Rainey, it included other blues singers, various novelty acts, comedians, and vaudeville performers. Because there were no microphones, performers of necessity had to have strong voices; the term "blues shouter" probably originates among these early performers because they literally had to "shout" to be heard. The band that played with the troupe was much like the groups that Ma later recorded with, consisting of drums, violin, bass, and trumpet. The Rabbit Foot Minstrels performed throughout the south and even into Mexico. Leib reports that the Rabbit Foot company was successful enough to travel in its own railroad car. Besides being an efficient way to travel, the train also eliminated the need to find accommodations in communities that relegated African Americans to inferior hotels or cheap boarding houses. All the descriptions of Ma Rainey report that she was short, heavy, and dark-skinned, and not particularly attractive in a conventional sense. She wore heavy jewelry that displayed diamonds and gold pieces, and she dressed in elaborate gowns. At the same time, Ma displayed an earthy sort of temperament and performance style that must have been attractive to her southern audience. Rainey worked with Bessie Smith in several touring companies between 1914 and 1916, and critics have acknowledged that Rainey was clearly an influence on the younger Bessie. How significant this influence was is a matter for debate and conjecture, but certainly the earliest Bessie Smith records show a more folk or rural influence than some of her later works. Similarly Rainey influenced the African American vaudeville-blues singing duo Butterbeans and Susie, who toured with her. It is likely that virtually all of the singers of the 1920s, especially those based in the south, had seen and heard Ma Rainey, and were influenced by her repertoire and enormously popular performing style. Rainey also had to function as a comedienne and a dancer in these touring shows.

Lovie Austin played piano and wrote several of Ma's recorded songs. Lovie was one of the few female musicians active in early jazz as well as blues. Later, Rainey's bandleader was Thomas A. Dorsey, renowned in subsequent years as a blues artist in his own right (performing as "Georgia Tom"), and later still, considered to be the father of black gospel music. Dorsey played piano, led the band, and wrote a number of Ma Rainey's recorded songs. The TOBA theaters were drastically affected by the introduction of sound into movies in the late 1920s, and the singers and other performers who earned the bulk of their income from touring shows found themselves scrambling for employment. Within a few years, the Great Depression hit the United States, and record sales plummeted as well. By 1928 Ma Rainey's recording career had ended. Paramount Records stopped recording the blues entirely by 1932, and in 1935, following the death of her sister, Ma Rainey returned to her home state of Georgia, where she managed two theaters and became active in the church. She died in 1939 at age 53.

We have already discussed the influence of Ma Rainey on other singers. Two other examples of her influence are worth mentioning. The black poet Sterling Brown wrote a poem about Ma Rainey, which describes one of her performances. It speaks of people coming to town from all around to see the show, from "blackbottom cornrows and lumber camps." The poem lists several of Rainey's favorite subjects, and continues

> I talked to a fellow, an' the fellow say,
> "She 'jes catch hold of us, somekindaway."

This sentiment surely reflected what so many of Ma Rainey's audience felt about their lives.

In 1940, 6 months after Ma Rainey's death, singer-guitarist Memphis Minnie recorded a tribute to Rainey. It contains the lines

> She was born in Georgia, traveled all over this world;
> And she's the best blues singer, peoples, I ever heard.

Minnie concludes with the lines

> People it sure look lonesome since Ma Rainey been gone,
> But she left little Minnie to carry the good works on.

There is a tradition of songs honoring blues singers after their death, but what is particularly interesting in this song is Minnie's assertions that Ma was the best blues singer that she ever heard, and her reference to Rainey's "good works." It is worth mentioning that Memphis Minnie, as we see below, was very much rooted in the male folk-blues tradition, rather than the cabaret mode of performance. This confirms Leib's notion that Rainey's work was close in spirit to the folk blues.

Unfortunately, from the standpoint of creating a legacy, Rainey was poorly served by Paramount Records. Rainey's records have been reissued on LP, and more recently on CD, but the audio quality is very poor, to the point where it is a little difficult to listen to them, particularly or to understands the words of the songs. It would be wonderful if one of the reissue companies would devote the sort of attention to restoring these poorly recorded works that has been devoted to the reissued works of Bessie Smith and Robert Johnson.

BESSIE SMITH: EMPRESS OF THE BLUES

If Ma Rainey had her feet in the folk tradition, even though she was a professional performer, Bessie Smith (1894–1937) straddled the line between blues and cabaret music. Bessie started recording in 1923, just prior to Ma Rainey's work with Paramount Records. Although Bessie was born in Chattanooga, Tennessee, she performed in Atlantic City even before her recording career began. Sometimes Bessie lived with her husband Jack Gee in Philadelphia, or in an apartment that she rented in New York.

Bessie's recording career began under the auspices of songwriter pianist Clarence Williams, who introduced her to record producer

Frank Walker, who was a staff producer for Columbia Records. She was initially paid $125 a side for her recordings, with no songwriting or artist royalties. Williams somehow managed to take half of this money, until Bessie and her husband complained to Frank Walker. When Walker arranged for her to get the entire advance, Bessie was so impressed that she asked him to be her manager. Walker agreed, overlooking his possible conflict of interest in representing both Bessie and her record company. During the height of her career Bessie's fees were upped to $200 per side, still without royalty payments of any kind.

Most of what we know about Bessie Smith comes from Chris Albertson's biography of her, which has recently been reprinted in a revised edition. A great deal of the information in the Albertson book comes from Bessie's niece, Ruby Walker, and Bessie's sister-in-law, Maud Walker. The research for this book was carried out more than 35 years after Bessie's death, so that many of the details of her life and career cannot be entirely recreated. Nevertheless, Albertson has done an excellent job of capturing the musical and social world of Bessie Smith.

Bessie was a woman with a huge appetite for life. Both Bessie and Ma Rainey were unapologetically bisexual, which was rather unusual for the time. Bessie was also "fond of her gin," and by all accounts could become violent when she didn't get exactly what she wanted. That could be alcohol, men, or women, depending on her mood and the circumstances. Her life was a study in ambivalence — varying between vulnerability and aggressiveness. Her relationship with her husband Jack Gee tended toward extremes of love and hate, and there was a considerable amount of physical violence between the two of them. Gee is credited with composing several of Bessie's songs, and many authors have speculated that these composer credits were gifts from Bessie to appease her high-living husband, because Jack had no musical background or apparent talent.

Albertson claims that Bessie appealed to both white and black audiences, and to some extent she was the darling of that odd breed of New York socialite typified by writer-photographer Carl Van Vechten. Van Vechten invited her to his upscale parties, and flattered her in a rather patronizing manner. In some of the southern locales where Bessie performed, theaters would have one or more shows a week where white audiences were invited. According to

Albertson, Bessie's huge voice and good diction proved as appealing to white audiences as to black ones. Bessie appeared in numerous Broadway reviews, and was generally well received by the critics.

Smith's career faded by the mid-1930s, and she was reduced to touring small towns in the south. In 1937, her life ended tragically while she was on the road. For years there was a popular story that Bessie Smith bled to death by the side of the road in Mississippi after being in an automobile accident. The story maintained that an ambulance refused to take the singer to a white hospital, and that the delay resulted in her bleeding to death. However, biographer Albertson determined that this story was fabricated on flimsy evidence by noted record producer John Hammond. Apparently the ambulance never went to the white hospital, and Smith's injuries were so severe that a similar accident might have killed her today, even with all of the medical advances of the last 70 years. The legend became so ingrained in the reminiscences of Bessie Smith that playwright Edward Albee constructed a play around it, called *The Death of Bessie Smith.*

THE RECORDINGS AND IMPORTANCE OF BESSIE SMITH

Bessie Smith had a long and successful recording career. However, she profited little from her recordings; according to Albertson, her entire income from Columbia Records was $28,575 dollars, representing payment for 160 different recordings. Bessie's recording of *Downhearted Blues,* her bestselling record, sold 780,000 copies in the first 6 months. It would be interesting to know how many copies were sold of Bessie's entire catalog. If we add to this the reissue LPs and CDs, and all of the various foreign releases, it becomes very clear that Bessie's work created quite a bonanza for Columbia Records.

Edward Brooms has written a record-by-record musical analysis of all of Bessie Smith's recordings, called *The Bessie Smith Companion.* It is his contention that Bessie used many musical skills in achieving the artistry of her recordings. Among her musical mannerisms he lists

- Unusual breath control
- Skilled harmonic sense that enabled her to slide up and down different notes of chords

- Excellent diction
- Clever use of musical dynamics
- Strong sense of pitch
- Ability to improvise
- Creative use of melisma — the singing of several notes on a single syllable of text

Brooks also found that in a number of Bessie's recordings, the band starts at one tempo, and she actually forces them to slow the tempo down — showing her tremendous control over her material. This may be one reason why Bessie never recorded with a drummer, with the single exception of one 1931 session, and the soundtrack for her *St. Louis Blues* film. It is virtually impossible to imagine any contemporary blues singer, particularly a "shouter," recording in the twenty-first century without a drummer!

Bessie's recordings have several advantages over those of Ma Rainey. First, the sound quality is much better. Columbia adopted the use of electrical recording in 1925, which Paramount never did. This involved the use of microphones, producing better-quality sound, and better balance between the singer and her accompanists. If anything, this is even more apparent in reissue recordings than on the original 78 rpm issues. The quality of Bessie's accompanists was also, generally speaking, better than that of the musicians who played on Ma Rainey's records. Louis Armstrong and Joe Smith, in particular, were inspired cornet players, and Charley Green on trombone was an excellent foil for Bessie.

Columbia dropped Bessie Smith's contract in 1931, after lowering her fee back to the original $125 a side. In 1933 John Hammond financed a Columbia recording session with Bessie out of his own pocket, but he reduced Smith's fee to $37.50 a side. Bessie refused to sing any blues, and sang four vaudeville-tinged songs. The musicians who played on the record included underrated trumpet star Frankie Newton, the young (white) trombonist Jack Teagarden, tenor sax player Chu Berry, and even a guest appearance by Benny Goodman. These recordings were not released until years later, and Bessie continued to do shows in New York and Philadelphia. A 1937 southern tour resulted in the automobile acci-dent and her death.

The influence of Bessie Smith continued long after her death. When the blues revival of the 1960s started, white blues singers such as Janis Joplin and Tracy Nelson had clearly listened long and hard to her recordings. Joplin, in fact, helped finance a gravestone for Bessie's unmarked grave in Philadelphia. Not surprisingly, Albertson reports that John Hammond contributed $50, which he charged to his Columbia expense account; the company itself contributed nothing. Albertson's biography of Bessie first appeared in 1973, with a revised edition appearing 30 years later. Columbia has reissued all of her recordings, and Frog, a small British company, has even reissued all of the alternative unissued takes.

HE DONE ME WRONG: CLASSIC BLUES SUBJECTS

If you purchase the numerous reissue recordings of various blues singers, you will notice that in many cases there are no composer credits, and often the dates of the recordings are not given. The lack of song credits often occurs because the songs were bought outright by the record companies or record producers. In some cases, there is no record of who wrote the songs. There are even two massive collections of blues lyrics edited by Eric Sackheim and Michael Taft that list the artists' names without listing songwriting credits. We are therefore fortunate that Angela Davis has reprinted the lyrics of all the songs recorded by Ma Rainey and Bessie Smith in her book *Blues Legacies and Black Feminism,* and has also included composer credits with each song. My analysis of the songs is based on the lyrics reprinted by Davis, which must represent hundreds of hours of listening.

Before we get into the actual song lyrics, it would be useful to go over some of the points that Davis makes about the context of the blues. Prior to the end of slavery, African Americans had no ability to travel, unless the master took them on a trip. They had no political or economic rights. From the owner's point of view, the purpose of sex between slaves was simply to breed the best possible slaves. If the master wished to assert his own sexual claims on black women, it was a given that he had that prerogative. The master was the caretaker, and any choices regarding the slave's physical or mental well-being belonged to him. Any religious, educational, or musical activities existed at the pleasure of the owner, and could be eliminated if they posed any real or imagined threat to the institution of slavery. This is not to deny that slaves created their own informal network of education, religion, or music, but to emphasize how dependent these options were on the choices made by the master.

When slavery ended, the slaves were thrust suddenly into a position of being responsible for their own lives and behaviors. They could choose their sexual outlets (as long as they didn't involve whites), and they could travel freely. In practice only men could avail themselves of this opportunity, although certainly the classic blues women of the 1920s did considerable traveling from one town to another in the course of their performances. The newly freed slaves were now also responsible for their own economic well-being, their housing, food, and medical care.

There was also a marked difference in attitude between the content of blues songs, and the nineteenth-century spirituals and the later gospel songs. The religious songs focused on the afterlife, where good behavior would be rewarded and bad behavior punished. Thus, religious music provided the security of definite answers — even if these answers were not available during the singer's lifetime. The blues, on the other hand, were about everyday behaviors, and its "profane" subjects included sex, violence, dances, partying, traveling, and working. The blues were about questions and ambivalence, rather than answers or the mediation of a Greater Power. "I may be wrong, but I'll be right someday," for example, is an assertion of individuality, not a plea for divine intervention.

So what subjects did the classic female blues performers address? By far the majority of both Ma Rainey's and Bessie Smith's material dealt with "no good" (or cheating) men. While these songs are felt by some to focus on the female's suffering and powerlessness in sexual relationships, they also asserted women's strength and independence. Often, the female threatens the philandering mate, either with physical violence or with the not-so-veiled threat of leaving him for a more reliable man.

There is some ambivalence in both singers' attitudes towards men. Some of this is the notion of payback: "You treated me wrong but I'll get back at you." This could be considered an assertion of independence or a rationalization. The question of faithfulness also is an issue that brings forth ambiguity and rationalization. The singers often take the position that there are "many fish in the sea;" in other words, you messed around with other women so I will mess around too. Because Ma's following, in particular, was largely in the south, there may have been a strong element of identification for the female listeners — who may well have wished that they had the financial wherewithal and the easy opportunities that were available to a traveling performer to play around with men other than their boyfriends or husbands.

However, both Rainey and Smith recorded songs that dealt with issues beyond romantic love and jealousy. Smith, in particular, dealt with a wider range of material, recording many songs that weren't technically "blues" although Columbia marketed her as a blues singer. The greater variety of subjects available to Bessie through her songwriters may have reflected the extensive time she spent in the New York area, and her lengthier recording career. Bessie undoubtedly felt some pressure to record other sorts of songs besides blues, particularly later in her career, when she performed in the same jazz clubs as younger singers such as Billie Holiday.

OTHER BLUES WOMEN OF THE 1920s

There were literally dozens of women who recorded blues songs during the 1920s, some making only a single 78, others prolifically composing and performing. The following were some of the more important singers of this period:

- Lucille Bogan (1897–1948. Bogan also used the name Bessie Jackson). In a group of women who used outspokenly bawdy lyrics, Bogan was possibly the most sexually oriented of them all. Her songs discussed such steamy subjects as adultery, lesbianism, and prostitution. Bogan wrote most of her own songs.
- Ida Cox (1896–1967). Like many of the classic blues singers, Cox began her career by touring with a minstrel show. Her song *Wild Women Don't Have the Blues* is very popular among young white blues singers today. Inactive for over 20 years, Cox recorded a final album in 1961.
- Lucille Hegamin (1894–1970). Hegamin used the name The Georgia Peach which was probably an attempt to capitalize on her beauty. Like Cox, she also recorded an album years after her career had seemingly ended.
- Bertha "Chippie" Hill (1905–1950). Hill was another vaudeville performer, but more of a blues singer than many of her peers. She left the music business in order to raise seven children, but

had a renewed music career after her rediscovery by jazz historian Rudi Blesh in 1946.

- Alberta Hunter (1895–1984). A veteran vaudeville performer, Hunter was a talented singer and songwriter, whose songs were performed by many leading blues artists in the 1920s and 1930s. Hunter was quite entrepreneurial, and she actually solicited Bessie Smith's record producer to record her song *Downhearted Blues*, after Hunter's own version had run its course in record sales. After the blues era ended, Hunter left music to pursue a career as a nurse. Rediscovered in the late 1970s, she resumed her music career at the age of 82, enthusiastically recording and performing until her death.

- Lottie Kimbrough (ca. 1900–?). Kimbrough was from Kansas City, and she worked there through the 1920s. She disappeared from the music scene in 1930. Her brother Sylvester was also a recording artist.

- Clara Smith (1894–1935). One of the few classic singers who had a voice powerful enough to be considered on a par with the great Bessie Smith (no relation). Bessie was notoriously critical of other blues artists, but respected Clara well enough to record duets with her. Clara recorded 125 songs before her career was cut short by a heart attack.

- Mamie Smith (1883–1946). One of the least interesting blues singers of the classic period, Mamie's primary historical importance rests on two factors. She was the first black artist to record a blues song, and her second record, *Crazy Blues*, sold over a million copies, and was responsible for virtually all record companies becoming interested in the blues.

- Trixie Smith (1895–1943). Trixie simply wanted to sing in theaters until she won a blues contest in 1922. Her most interesting blues seemed to have been about trains, especially her *Freight Train Blues*, recorded in 1938. She also appeared in one film and had bit parts in several Broadway shows. Trixie, Clara, Bessie, and Mamie — while sharing the same surname — were not related.

- Victoria Spivey (1906–1976). Spivey was a songwriter and a good business woman; she was a contract composer even before she was a recording artist. She is best known for her songs *T.B. Blues and Black Snake Moan*. The latter was a source of argument between Spivey and Blind Lemon Jefferson, because both claimed to have written it. Like many others, Spivey retired until the blues revival of the mid-1950s, when she began to record and perform. She started her own record company in 1962, recording herself, and some of her friends including Lucille Hegamin and Lonnie Johnson, and even a young Bob Dylan as a sideman on harmonica.

- Eva Taylor (1895–1977). Another vaudeville performer, Taylor moved to New York. She was married to songwriter-entrepreneur Clarence Williams, and she often appeared with him.

- Sippie Wallace (1898–1986). Wallace was a member of a very musical family. She often performed with her younger brother, the brilliant pianist Hersal, and her songwriting partner was her brother, George. Her career was greatly setback by Hersal's death in 1926, followed by George's passing in 1936. She turned to religion until Victoria Spivey convinced her to come out of out of retirement in 1966. In 1982, young white singer-songwriter Bonnie Raitt helped Sippie Wallace get a deal with Atlantic Records, and produced her "comeback" album. Wallace's song *Women Be Wise, Don't Advertise Your Man* remains popular among women blues revivalists.

- Edith Wilson (1896–1981). Wilson was a sophisticated cabaret singer and comedienne, capable of acting and singing on Broadway, and even in London. She toured France several times, singing in French as well as in English. She retired in 1963, but a 1972 comeback brought her performances and a final album.

While dozens of books about the blues are available, there is only one real survey of the classic "blues queens" of the 1920s: Daphne Duval Harrison's *Black Pearls: Blues Queens Of the 1920s*. So much of the current vogue for the blues stems from the use of delta blues style in rock and roll that blues enthusiasts (and scholars) may find the majority of the classic female singers lack the emotional intensity they feel is the hallmark of the blues. It is true that many of these singers came out of a cabaret, vaudeville, or theatrical background, and some drifted back in that direction after the blues boom of the 1920s faded away. We should probably distinguish between the artists who were songwriters and those for whom the blues was essentially a vehicle for achieving pop-music success. Mamie Smith, Lucille Hegamin, and Edith Wilson, for example, were essentially cabaret singers for whom the blues was simply a part of their repertoire. Alberta Hunter, Ida Cox, and Victoria Spivey went back and forth between the styles, but all of them returned to the blues. This may have been due partially to the extraordinary length of their musical careers, and to the fact that the blues revival of the 1960s created opportunities for these singers to find renewed employment opportunities.

The blues revival tended to focus on blues singers who were also instrumentalists; this may be a reason why the classic female singers did not receive recognition. Spivey and Wallace did play piano, but Wallace, who came from a family of musicians, only played on a few of her own recordings. Spivey was a prolific songwriter. Her *T.B. Blues, Black Snake Moan, and No. 12 Let Me Roam* were all songs that other artists performed and recorded; *Black Snake* was a big hit for Blind Lemon Jefferson, and Josh White recorded and performed the other songs. But again the blues revivalists liked to focus on the songs themselves as being "traditional," so her songwriting credits were often overlooked.

And, of course, the sexism in the music world cannot be overlooked. Most women are expected to stay at home, or to pursue traditional careers (such as nursing, as Alberta Hunter did in later years). Being a traveling musician — particularly performing music as often off-color and rowdy as the blues — is not considered to be an appropriate lifestyle for women. Most of the fans of rural blues were male, and so the blues revivalists went in search of the male singers of the 1920s and 1930s. The more urban stylings of female performers were recognized by some fans of early jazz or even cabaret singing, but these fans did not crossover into the blues revival. All of this may have contributed to the lack of attention that these female blues singers have received.

WOMEN AND THE FOLK BLUES

Memphis Minnie was a superb guitarist, singer, and songwriter who generally recorded with another guitarist. We discuss her work in Chapter 3, because although her first recordings were made in 1929, it was during the 1930s and even later that her career flourished. Minnie was not the only woman who performed in a country-folk style, although she is by far the best known. The lesser-known Geeshie Wiley and Mattie Delaney were also guitarists, singers, and songwriters.

JAZZ INFLUENCES ON THE BLUES

Most of the classic blues singers used small jazz combos on their recordings. The band would usually consist of a horn or two, tuba often substituted for the string bass, and piano was common. Oddly, Bessie Smith almost never used drums on her recordings. Although blues are considered to be an essential ingredient of jazz, jazz blues are somewhat different from folk blues. Songs often are in 16 and 32 bar patterns rather than 12 bars, and often the chords used are more complex than the I–IV–V progressions found in the folk blues. In later years the chords became increasingly complicated, and used a musical device called "chord substitutions." This means that the musician or musical arranger would use other chords in place of the simple progressions. A typical example would be to place IIm and IIIm chords between the I and the IV. In the key of C instead of the progression going C to F, it becomes C–Dm–Em–F. Another sort of substitution is in modifying the I–IV–V chords by adding 6ths, 9ths, or other notes (for a C chord this is an A, and a D an octave higher). Other, more complicated chords also were used, especially when swing gave way to bebop in the mid-1940s.

Summary
The classic blues singers were not folk artists, but professional singers who had extensive performing experiences. Many of their recordings used jazz musicians as accompanists. Although Ma Rainey and Bessie Smith were the most famous classic blues artists, the listener will be rewarded by paying attention to the works of such other artists as Ida Cox and Sippie Wallace. These female blues singers have not enjoyed the popularity and attention they deserve among blues fans.

3

THE FOLK BLUES:
1920–1940

TIMELINE: 1920–1940

TIMELINE: 1920–1940

1924	Daddy Stovepipe and Papa Charlie Jackson made their first recordings, the first folk blues performers to appear on disc
1926	Blind Lemon Jefferson made his first records
1929	U.S. stock market crash led to world depression, precipitous decline in record sales
	Charley Patton recorded
1932	Franklin Delano Roosevelt elected U.S. president
1933	Hitler named Chancellor of Germany
1935	First recorded electric guitar music (Eddie Durham)
1936–37	Robert Johnson recorded
1939	World War II began

AFRICAN AMERICAN MUSICAL STYLES

Although the first popular recordings of the blues occurred in 1920, the earliest blues music differs in a number of ways from the so-called classic blues. First, let us review the African American music styles that were present in 1920. These styles include:

- *Traditional hollers*: Unaccompanied work songs sung while working.

- *Work songs*: Same as above, but sung by groups of people, rather than individuals.
- *Folk or "Down Home" blues*: Blues songs performed usually by traveling singers accompanying themselves on guitar for a folk/rural audience.
- *Holy blues*: Songs that utilize blues melodies and instrumental techniques, but contain religious words.
- *Ragtime*: Primarily instrumental music played on piano or banjo; later the guitar is substituted for the banjo. Note that popular songwriters, white and black, were integrating ragtime into commercial pop music.
- *Hokum and jug band music*: Music utilizing a combination of homemade instruments such as the jug or washtub bass and banjos, banjo-mandolin, fiddle, and kazoo. This music was a sort of simplified version of ragtime, with blues elements as well.
- *Classic blues*: A marriage of the blues and vaudeville-theatrical musical styles, sung by women (see Chapter 2).
- *Jazz*: Syncopated band music, mostly performed by African Americans, although there were some white artists.
- *Spirituals*: Religious songs, performed in churches, and on the concert stage by touring black choirs.
- *String band music*: This music was influenced by both ragtime and country music. Many of the professional black musicians performed for white as well as black audiences, and also had some musical contact with white musicians.

The reader should understand that there were a number of black musicians, such as the Mississippi-based Chatmon Brothers, whose music crossed all of these lines. These musicians might perform, in no particular sequence, jug band music, string band music, blues, ragtime, and jazz-influenced tunes, as well as the pop tunes of the day.

In this chapter, we will primarily focus on the folk blues and related styles, including hokum and jug band music, holy blues, and string band music.

WHY THE CLASSIC BLUES WERE RECORDED BEFORE THE FOLK BLUES

The record companies initially had no idea that there was any demand at all for black music. They assumed that blacks were too poor to be able to afford to buy phonographs, and to purchase records on a regular basis. They also (somewhat correctly at the time) assumed that the white population would have no interest in black musical styles or performances. Their minds were changed primarily because a number of black songwriter-musicians-entrepreneurs kept pestering the record executives to record black music. These black entrepreneurs, including Perry Bradford and Clarence Williams, were urban-based songwriters and musicians, and probably had little or no familiarity with folk blues styles in 1920. They wanted to further their own careers, so it was only natural that they pressed the record companies to record their songs performed by artists whom they either were managing or had some financial interest in. When Bessie Smith's recordings achieved popularity, the record companies all jumped on the bandwagon, and sought to find other professional female singers who performed in a style similar to that already on record. Bradford and Williams were quick to bring these singers to the attention of record companies, and to cut themselves in on the action by writing songs and playing on the recording sessions.

Once record companies started to pursue field recordings as an alternative to big city studio recordings, it was inevitable that they would record folk blues artists. In 1923, Ralph Peer, then director of recording for Okeh Records, and soon to defect to RCA Victor, traveled to Atlanta to record country fiddler Fiddlin' John Carson. Peer took portable recording equipment, and, according to Jeff Todd Titon, writing in his book *Down Home Blues*, Peer may have recorded Birmingham blues singer Lucille Bogan at the same time. (It is not clear whether she was recorded on this trip, or at studios in Chicago or New York.) Subsequent folk blues recordings (Titon favors the term *down home blues*) took place in 1924. Although Daddy Stovepipe was recorded first, it was the recordings of Papa Charlie Jackson for Paramount Records that achieved exposure and popularity. Jackson played the six-string banjo (called a banjo-guitar, because it was tuned like a guitar but had the body of a banjo) and performed in a sort of semi-vaudeville hokum style. His records included a sort of verbal commentary that owed more to vaudeville than to the blues. He also recorded some tunes with Ma Rainey, which are in the form of joking conversations between them, with virtually as much dialogue as music.

BLIND LEMON JEFFERSON

The first folk blues "star" was Blind Lemon Jefferson. We do not have much information about Lemon's life, but we know that he was born, according to which book you believe, in 1893 or 1897 in a small town about 70 miles south of Dallas. Lemon was blind at birth, and by the time he was a teenager he was navigating his way through various Texas towns, picking up tips as a street musician. It was not unusual for blind men to take up music as a means of supporting themselves; unable to work at more conventional jobs, they were reduced to begging for tips. By 1917, Jefferson had moved to Dallas. Among the young boys who helped Jefferson to collect his tips on the streets of Dallas were Huddie (Leadbelly) Ledbetter and T. Bone Walker, both destined to go on to distinguished musical careers. (In the 1940s, Leadbelly recorded a song about Blind Lemon in which he talks about the two of them hitching rides on trains, working their way through small Texas towns.) Jefferson accompanied himself on guitar, and often the guitar was like a second voice, providing answers to the lyrics of his songs.

Writing in his book *Big Road Blues*, David Evans points out that, when Jefferson began his recording career in 1926, almost half of Lemon's recorded songs were traditional: 13, against 16 that Jefferson claimed to have composed. By 1929, there were 22 original compositions and no traditional ones. This brings up an interesting issue. Many blues singers had a repertoire that largely consisted of traditional songs. Obviously it would be impossible for record companies to keep issuing the same songs by the same, or for that matter, other artists, and expect that the public would continue to buy multiple versions of them. There were also monetary motivations on the part of the record company, or the record producers. When Ralph Peer joined RCA Victor in the later 1920s as a house producer, his deal with the company stipulated that he would not be paid anything for producing records, but that he could retain the publishing rights to any songs that he recorded. Consequently, Peer had no interest in recording traditional music, because he would not be paid for doing so.

Many of the early blues singers were not only untutored musicians, but were also illiterate or semiliterate. They would have difficulty in writing down their own songs, and thus would have to remember them. Under these circumstances, it was difficult for them to keep coming up with fresh material. Lemon did not seem to have these difficulties, recording 16 original songs in 1927, 17 in 1927, 20 in 1928, and 22 in 1929.

Lemon's entree into the record business came through the owner of a Dallas music store, who arranged for Lemon to travel to Chicago to record for Paramount. His record producer was an African American, J. Mayo Williams, who worked for Paramount and over the years produced dozens of other blues artists. Jefferson was sufficiently successful that Williams bought him a $700 car. When Williams moved over to Okeh Records, he brought Jefferson along with him, a questionable legal maneuver because Jefferson was under contract to Paramount. Paramount responded by bringing Jefferson back to the studio.

The songs recorded by the classic female blues singers of the 1920s were mostly songs that had a definite structure, and told a coherent story. Many of Lemon's songs, and those of other folk blues artists, were much more loosely constructed. It is important to remember that the artist was sitting in an (often unfamiliar) recording studio environment. There were absolute time limitations on songs, which were recorded not on tape but direct to disc. When the disc was close to running out of time, a red light would flash to inform the singer that he needed to end the song. If the performer, like Lemon, was blind, then someone would tap him on the shoulder to indicate that time was running out. Under those circumstances, the singer was under pressure to deliver a song of specific length. Because the typical blues format had repeated lines, such as AAB or ABB, often the singer would come into the session with the first line in his mind, and would make up the second line while the first line was repeated. Often one verse would not specifically relate to the previous verse, or the singer might contradict himself from one verse to another. The singer/performer would often draw on standard verses to fill out a song; because these verses often appeared in many different songs, scholars call them "floating verses."

What are we to make of these lyric shifts? In my opinion, the best way to analyze these flights of fancy is to imagine that they are simply snapshots of what is going through the singer's mind. There are many of Jefferson's songs that do not have a coherent story line, but use verses that function as commentaries on a particular subject. Scholars generally feel that the primary subject of blues is the relationship between men and women, so many blues, and Lemon's blues in particular, start out with a specific subject, say the war (such as in his *Wartime Blues*), and shift over into various commentaries on specific woman friends, or women in general. Often the lyrics are ambivalent, with the singer denying the importance of a specific girlfriend, and then later expressing a yearning for her (e.g., in Jefferson's *Corinna Blues*). Or the singer may shift his attention in the song from one woman to another.

Lemon's subject matter varied widely. Several of his songs were about jail, or prison experiences, such as *Prison Cell Blues*, *'Lectric Chair Blues*, *Blind Lemon's Penitentiary Blues*, and *Hangman's Blues*. Other songs concerned current events, such as *Wartime Blues*, *Oil Well Blues*, *Christmas Eve Blues*, or *Happy New Year*. There are also a number of religious songs in Jefferson's work, including *See That My Grave's Kept Clean* and *He Arose from the Dead*. Among Lemon's earliest recordings were two songs recorded under the name "Deacon J. Bates." This was probably done so that a separate market might be created for the religious side of Lemon's work, but apparently when Lemon had become something of a star, this ploy was abandoned by Paramount. The subject of women and physical love is by far Lemon's favorite, as you can see if you listen to the 94 songs on the four reissued CDs in the JSP Records boxed set of Lemon's work. This is a pattern that, as we will see, is mirrored in the work of most other folk blues singers. Toward the end of this chapter, we will undertake a more detailed discussion of the lyric content of the blues.

The two dominant musical styles found in folk blues are the intense and emotional Mississippi Delta style, and the ragtimeish style found in the Carolinas and Georgia, usually referred to as Piedmont style. Lemon was from Texas, and his music stands midway between these two musical styles. There is more single-string playing than in either of the other styles, and there is not an obvious single dominant musical characteristic in Texas blues. There are only two songs where another musician plays on Lemon's records, both featuring piano accompaniment by pianist George Perkins. The fidelity of Lemon's recordings is poor, say in comparison to the work of Bessie Smith. In both of the recordings where

Thomas plays, it is barely possible to hear Lemon's guitar. The only other "musical" addition to Jefferson's work is his own foot stomping on an instrumental with a recitation entitled *Hot Dogs*. This is an unusual piece for Jefferson, almost a ragtime-styled instrumental of the sort that Blind Blake recorded.

Lemon's guitar playing has a tendency to speed up or slow down, something that Mississippi blues artist Son House criticized. The fact is that because Lemon almost always played solo, he functioned in much the same way that a solo folksinger works, adjusting the rhythm to his own moods or to the lyrics of a particular song. It is easy to imagine that dancers had some difficulties dancing with any sort of ease to Lemon's work because of the shifting tempos.

Nonetheless, Lemon was a powerful guitar player. Some of the techniques that he used are slapping the bass strings, using the guitar to answer the lyrics to represent almost a human voice, and occasionally playing a sort of contrapuntal rhythm against the melody and sung-lyric of a song. Many of these instrumental answers are played at high speed, and are difficult to execute accurately. Most of Blind Lemon's music utilizes the three primary chords in a key (C or C7, F or F7, and G7 in the key of C). Other songs use the typical ragtime progression of I–VI7–II7–V–I, or C–A7–D7–G7–C in the key of C.

Blind Lemon Jefferson was an important influence among blues singers, and his influence was felt for some years. Country-rockabilly singer Carl Perkins covered Lemon's *Matchbox Blues* and later The Beatles also recorded it. In effect, Blind Lemon opened the door for the raft of folk blues artists who followed, and he also was an important influence on the blues revival that took place more than 30 years after his death.

THE JUG BANDS

Jug bands are bands that contain a variety of homemade or jerry-rigged instruments, such as jugs, combs, washtub basses, washboards, and kazoos, along with harmonicas, banjos, fiddles, mandolins, tenor guitars, or guitars. The banjos involved vary from the five-string "folk" banjo, to the four-string tenor banjo more common in Dixieland jazz, and the banjo-mandolin. The tenor banjo is a more effective rhythm instrument than the five string, and its shorter scale and higher tuning tends to have a brighter sound, which is effective in cutting through the jug band instruments. The banjo-mandolin is basically a mandolin with a skin head (like a banjo) that is tuned and played like a mandolin. The tenor guitar is a four-string guitar with a higher pitched sound than the normal six-string guitar.

The musical style of jug band music is generally medium to up-tempo, and the mood is generally happy, and even jocular. Seemingly it is at the opposite pole from the slower, deeper, introspective sort of style that characterizes Delta blues. On the other hand, jug band music is a sort of close relative to the Piedmont blues, which also tend to be positive in lyric content, and medium to up-tempo in rhythm. This was definitely good-time party music, and it is easy to understand its appeal to people of all races and ages.

Memphis seems to have been one of the leading incubators of jug band music. Memphis stands at a sort of peculiar geographic juxtaposition as a destination town for emigrants from the Mississippi delta, but also not too distant from the Carolinas or eastern Tennessee. Possibly more than any other city, Memphis was home to both the Delta blues styles and the more gentle ragtime-oriented music of the Piedmont region.

The Memphis Jug Band was led by guitarist-singer Will Slade, and it recorded from 1928 to 1934. During this period the band recorded almost a hundred titles. They performed at a variety of functions for both black and white audiences. Ethnomusicologist David Evans, writing in Lawrence Cohn's collection *Nothing but the Blues*, describes venues for jug bands as varying from working for tips in city parks, to birthday parties at private homes, store openings, medicine shows, tourist venues such as riverboats and excursion trains, and clubs on Beale Street in Memphis. The repertoire of the Memphis Jug Band and other such groups included string band instrumentals, ragtime pieces, pop songs of the day, and light blues.

The other notable Memphis Jug Band was Cannon's Jug Stompers, featuring the five-string banjo of Gus Cannon. Cannon played jug, as well as banjo, but the instrumental star of the band was soulful harmonica player Noah Lewis. The repertoire of the Stompers was similar to that of the Memphis Jug Band. Cannon's song *Walk Right In* became a tremendous pop hit when it was recorded in 1963 by the folk-pop group The Rooftop Singers.

There were other jug bands in Memphis, and such bands could also be found in Cincinnati and Louisville. There is even a record by an obscure religious performer, Rev. E.S. "Shy" Moore, which includes a jug in the instrumental accompaniment. Other musicians recorded with jug as part of the backing group. Although the jug band tradition mostly disappeared in the 1930s, the spirit of jug band music survived in the early 1940s group the Spirits of Rhythm, and the jocular performances of such artists as Louis Jordan and Slim Gaillard. During the 1960s, the folk revival sparked a number of (white) jug bands, such as Jim Kweskin's Jug Band and the Even Dozen Jug Band.

DELTA BLUES

When most people think of the folk blues today, they think of the Delta blues style, because they have been the most popular among revivalists and scholars. The Delta blues style is the one that has been most appealing to the rock and roll musicians who were influenced by the blues. Such players as Keith Richard of the Rolling Stones and Eric Clapton frankly acknowledge their debt to the delta musicians, especially Robert Johnson. That particular stream of delta music comes from around Clarksdale, particularly Dockery's Plantation near Cleveland, Mississippi. This was the home of Charley Patton, as well as a decade or so later of a young musician named McKinley Morganfeld (who became known as Muddy Waters when he moved to Chicago in the late 1940s).

CHARLEY PATTON

Charley Patton was one of 12 children, and his father was a preacher. He was a farmworker as a child, which may have accounted for his lack of enthusiasm for hard labor. He is known to have worked with Tommy Johnson, and as a soloist in various parts of Mississippi during the 1920s. Other than his recordings, made in New York from 1930 to 1934, Patton for the most part stayed around Mississippi. In this respect he differed from other Delta performers such as Son House and Robert Johnson.

Patton was a major figure in the evolution, if not the very origin, of Delta blues. Of course, we do not know much of anything about his predecessors, but there are a number of things that Patton brought to Delta blues style. First of all, he was in effect a teacher. Son House, Willie Brown, and to some extent Robert Johnson were influenced by his style of playing the guitar, and his method of entertaining. He supposedly performed lots of guitar tricks, such as playing the guitar behind his back and between his knees. There are similarities between Patton's way of thumping the bass strings with his thumb and the playing of Son House. Furthermore House's intense and loud singing style seems to be derived from Patton's vocals. Of course, there are differences between these two artists; although much has been made of Patton's influence on Son House, Son's guitar work is much more intense, almost raw. He often strummed down across the strings using a technique almost like a southern mountain banjo player — which is not at all like Patton's playing.

Patton also pursued a reckless lifestyle filled with womanizing, drinking, and feasting; it is not inconceivable that Robert Johnson took Patton as kind of a role model. Neither of them wanted to do anything but play music. At the time this must have seemed almost subversive to the average black farmer, for example. Although Johnson traveled more widely than Patton, they shared a disdain for physical labor and a love of performing — and all the "extras" that the life of a professional musician (money, women, drink) brought.

Although Patton is known today as a "blues performer," he really was more of a songster — performing a wide variety of material in addition to the blues. In Chapter 1, we briefly discussed the songster, a musician who had a broad repertoire that included blues, but also performed a range of other material, from folk ballads to pop songs. Many of the songsters, at least according to recorded evidence, were found in the Piedmont area and in Texas. Perhaps the most famous songster from Mississippi was John Hurt, who recorded a few sides in 1928 and was "rediscovered" during the blues revival of the 1960s.

It is important to remember that the line between "blues performer" and "songster" was often blurred. Performers themselves would play anything that was popular among their audience; after all, they were working the streets and hoping to get tips. In this light, it is interesting to compare Hurt with the Delta Blues legend Charley Patton, also from Mississippi. John Fahey points out in his groundbreaking book *Charley Patton* that Patton recorded many songs that were not really "blues," including ballads or story songs, ragtime songs, and many religious songs and spirituals. Fahey notes that some songs that contain the word "blues" in the titles are in fact not blues; he attributes this to the notion that neither record companies nor Patton himself had much interest in categorizing songs.

However, there is an important difference between Patton and a songster such as Mississippi John Hurt. Patton performed in an intense and emotional Delta style, with his guitar playing having a similar intensity, even on his religious songs. John Hurt brought a more relaxed style to his singing and guitar work, and took a lighter approach to his material, whether it was the blues song *Candy Man* or the ballad *Louis Collins*.

Although Patton was a songster who performed a variety of musical styles, a large percentage of his work focused on the blues. And his style, as we have noted, was markedly different from that of other songsters such as John Hurt. Sometimes he used a knife as a slide to note the strings, reproducing a crying moan or wail on the guitar. John Fahey's analysis of Patton's recordings show that he took a rather free-form approach to the structure of his music. Some of the verses of his songs did not contain 12 bars of music. Patton added or subtracted half a bar or even added parts of bars or entire bars, depending upon his mood or the way the lyrics flowed. It is the feeling of Patton's performances that distinguish his work — their rough edges (even the rough recording quality of the early 78s) contribute to his allure to the blues fan.

ROBERT JOHNSON: HIS LIFE, THE MUSIC, THE CONTROVERSIES, AND THE LEGEND

Of all the Delta musicians, Robert Johnson would ultimately be the most influential. This influence was not something that happened during his brief lifetime, but was a result of a series of odd circumstances that occurred long after his death. Johnson is believed to have been born in 1911, and was dead by 1938, only 27 years later. In his 2-year recording career, Robert recorded 29 selections, 24 of which were released on 78 rpm recordings during his lifetime.

Robert Johnson's life was an unusual one, from his birth until the day that he died. Robert was an illegitimate child whose mother was separated from her husband under peculiar circumstances. Julia Major Dodds was Robert's mother, and was married to Charles Dodds. According to Peter Guralnick, in his book *Searching for Robert Johnson*, Dodds was a successful maker of wicker furniture who also was a Mississippi landowner, and the couple had ten children. However, when Dodds got into an argument with some prominent local white landowners, he was forced to flee town, allegedly dressing in women's clothes in order to elude a lynch mob. He moved to Memphis, where he changed his name from Dodds to Spencer. Eight of the children made their way to Memphis and their father, but Julia stayed in Mississippi with two daughters. She took up with a plantation worker named Noah Johnson, and Robert was born to them. Guralnick writes that although Dodds eventually accepted Robert, he would never live with Julia again. By 1914, when Robert was 3 years old, his stepfather took him in, and he spent the next few years in Memphis. As a result of this early convoluted family life, Robert was variously known as Robert Dodd, Robert Spencer, Little Robert Dusty, and Robert Johnson. Julia eventually married Dusty Willis, and Robert returned to the Delta around 1918–1920, when he would have been between 7 and 9 years old.

According to Robert's contemporary Johnny Shines, Robert had little or no education, but Mississippi blues researcher Gayle Dean Wardlow found a record of his signature on two different marriage licenses. Wardlow, in his book *Chasin' That Devil Music*, described the signatures as "fluent and readable." So in or out of school, Robert had at least learned to sign his name.

Robert's first wife was Virginia Travis. They married in 1929, and by April 1930, she had died in childbirth, along with their unborn child. Robert later kept company with another woman, Vergie Mae Smith. She gave birth to a boy, but the couple split up and Robert then married an older woman named Calletta Craft. This marriage did not last long, although Craft claimed that on several occasions Robert returned and asked her to travel with him, but she refused these invitations. According to several other bluesmen, Robert often sought out older women who could "take care of him," providing food and lodging while he sang on street corners and in juke joints.

Robert had another significant relationship with Estella Coleman in Helena, Arkansas. She had a son named Robert Lockwood, and Johnson helped Lockwood learn how to play the guitar. In turn, he took the name "Junior" to honor Johnson; his original name was actually Robert Lockwood Jr.

Johnny Shines and Robert Jr. Lockwood — the two people who seemed to have known Robert best, or at least the ones who survived for some years to tell the story — described Robert as an inveterate wanderer, always ready to go from town to town, hitchhiking, riding the bus, or riding in the back of a farmer's wagon. He was also always looking for a woman to stay with, and sometimes this habit caused trouble, because Robert was not especially concerned about whether the woman was single or married. Johnny Shines was often interviewed about his travels with Robert, and he painted a picture of a wanderer who now and again would get into fights, altercations that left the two of them with bruises and broken bones.

Ultimately these habits led to Robert's death. He was playing in Friars Point, Mississippi, where he took up with a married woman. Her jealous husband supposedly poisoned him, and he died shortly afterwards. However, Wardlow found Robert's death certificate, which said that Robert died of "congenital syphilis." Wardlow also talked to a doctor named Walter Holladay, who suggested that the combination of poison, moonshine, and liver damage could have led to Robert's actually dying of pneumonia. The death certificate was dated August 16, 1938.

From an early age Robert played the harmonica and jews harp. His goal was to play the guitar, and in order to accomplish this he used the time-honored Delta tradition of hanging a wire on the wall of his house, and nailing the wire to the wall; the wire then acted like a guitar string. Robert used three strings, and from there he moved to an actual tenor (four-string) guitar, before finally settling on a six-string instrument. It happened that the local musicians included Son House and Willie Brown, both of whom were outstanding guitarists who went on to record. They discouraged Robert from playing guitar, telling him to stick to the harmonica. In interviews after his rediscovery in the 1960s, House remarked that Johnson's playing was so bad that, when Robert played while the duo was taking a break, people begged Robert to quit making a racket with his guitar playing.

Some time around 1930 Robert disappeared from the area, following his wanderlust. He was gone somewhere between 6 months and 2 years, depending upon which of Son House's later recollections one wants to believe. When he returned, Robert asked to sit in with the two musicians, and they agreed, expecting that they would have to get him to stop playing in short order. To their astonishment, they heard a new guitar player, one who they realized had gone beyond what they themselves were capable of playing. It is at this point that fact and legend diverge. Several researchers believe that Robert had moved south to the Hazlehurst area, and learned how to play guitar from a musician there named Ike Zinneman. Nonetheless, Robert's playing had made such great musical advances that the story arose that it was the devil himself who taught him, in exchange for possession of Robert's soul. We will take up the legend of Robert Johnson after we spend a little more time describing his musical career.

Apparently, from a fairly early time Robert Johnson had dreamed that he could become a recording star. As a teenager, he had told a Robinsonville friend named Elizabeth Glynn Moore that he would one day make records in New York. This was long before his emergence as a fine guitarist; in fact, Wardlow reports that, like Son House and Willie Brown, Moore had suggested to Robert that he stick to harmonica, because he made "constant mistakes" on the guitar.

The various books written about Robert Johnson are heavily indebted to various interviews with Johnny Shines. Shines described the two of them traveling as far as New York and Ontario, Canada, as well as various southern destinations. They played on street corners, in juke joints, at house parties, or wherever anyone would pay to hear them. Various musicians, such as Sonny Boy Williamson (#2) and Henry Townsend in St. Louis, remembered hearing Robert, and remarked on his musical talents. But Robert needed to find a way to make records, and through a Jackson, Mississippi, music store owner named H.C. Speir, he finally was able to achieve this goal.

Besides owning a music store that also sold records, Speir functioned as both a talent scout and artist and repertoire record producer for various recording companies. Among the Mississippi artists whom Speir recorded or discovered were Charley Patton,

Skip James, and Son House. Robert went to Jackson to see Speir in 1936. According to Peter Guralnick, by that time Speir had overseen the recording of almost 200 sides for the ARC label group, but they had only released 40 of them. Consequently, he elected to pass Robert to Ernie Oertle, a salesman and talent scout for ARC Records. Oertle heard Johnson, and agreed to take him to San Antonio to make records in November 1936.

The person who produced Robert Johnson's records was Don Law. Law was an English immigrant who had sung with the London Choral Society, and entered the record business as a bookkeeper. He later became a protégé of producer Art Satherly, and by the 1950s was the head of A&R at Columbia Records Nashville, where he produced a number of country music acts, including Marty Robbins and Lefty Frizzell.

Law's impression of Johnson was that he was shy and introverted, which may have been a function of the way Robert behaved around white people. It also may have been a response to the pressure of making his first recordings, and how much was riding on their success. Law rescued Robert from the local police, who roughed him up, accused him of vagrancy, and smashed his guitar. Later Robert summoned Law to help him again, this time because he wanted to borrow a nickel in order to pay a prostitute the 50-cent fee that she demanded. Law also told the story of how Robert was asked to play for some mariachi musicians who were also being recorded, and turned his back while playing for them. It is a matter of opinion (or conjecture) whether he turned his back out of shyness, or whether he simply was not interested in sharing his guitar techniques with other musicians.

All of Robert Johnson's biographers agree that Robert never achieved much in the way of commercial success during his lifetime. His first record release was *Terraplane Blues*, named after a current car model. It sold 5,000 copies, which was enough for ARC to want to continue to record Robert. No blues historian has reported exactly what the sales of Robert's subsequent recordings were, but all seem to agree that his first record was the biggest seller he ever had. If the record were being marketed today, we would probably look at it as a regional or even local hit that never spread elsewhere. Elijah Wald, in his book *Escaping the Delta: Robert Johnson and the Invention of the Blues*, states that it did show up on some Mississippi jukeboxes. However, Wald found few people in the Delta who remembered Robert, outside of some of his musical peers, a few friends, and his relatives, suggesting his success was rather limited. In the 3 days of recording during the San Antonio sessions, 16 selections were recorded, and 6 months later ARC brought Robert back, this time to Dallas, to record an additional 13 sides. These 29 songs, with some alternative takes, constitute the entire recorded legacy of Robert Johnson.

Oddly no blues scholar has asked what would appear to be the logical question: if subsequent recordings sold worse than *Terraplane Blues*, why did the company continue to record him? Did they feel that he had some commercial potential that was not being realized? Why would the company continue to invest money in a career that did not seem to be going anywhere in the middle of the Great Depression? Unfortunately, we will probably never know the answers to these questions, because everyone connected with the original sessions is now dead.

Before we discuss the contents of these songs, the lyrics, and the musical influences that Robert Johnson reflected, we will take a look at how the legend of Robert Johnson was born and developed, and why his name, so long dormant, has become a major part of blues history.

The legend of Robert Johnson probably can be traced to John Hammond's Carnegie Hall *Spirituals to Swing* concerts, presented in New York City in December 1938. Hammond was a record producer and a sort of all-music-styles talent scout for Columbia Records. Over the years he "discovered" jazz guitarist Charley Christian, jazz singer Billie Holiday, Bob Dylan, and Bruce Springsteen, among others. Hammond was also a lifelong liberal and believer in civil rights causes. In 1937, he wrote about Johnson's recordings for the left-wing periodical *New Masses*, extolling Johnson's virtues as an important blues singer. In the summer of 1938, Hammond presented a sort of kaleidoscopic history of jazz in a live Carnegie Hall concert. He wanted to include gospel music and blues as a sort of roots music examination of the backgrounds of jazz. Hammond had Don Law search for Robert Johnson, intending to bring him to the Carnegie Hall concert. Ultimately Ernie Oertle informed Law that Johnson was dead, and Hammond ended up using Big Bill Broonzy as his representative blues singer. But Hammond also went to the unusual and dramatic extreme of playing two of Robert's recordings at the concert, preceding them with an announcement of Johnson's death, and a spoken elegy on his life, which was later published in *New Masses*.

Despite Hammond's efforts, Robert Johnson's name began to disappear into obscurity, which is where it stayed until 1961. It is true that a few of Robert's songs, such as *Dust My Broom*, recorded in a very successful version by Elmore James, survived, but apart from some of Johnson's peers, such as James, Son House, Johnny Shines, and Robert Jr Lockwood, no one paid much attention.

Once again John Hammond played a significant role in bringing Johnson's work to light. During the late 1950s and up until about the mid-1960s, the United States experienced a folk music revival, which also brought a new interest in the blues, this time from a young white audience. Samuel Charters, one of the first blues scholars to write about the blues, included Robert's *Preaching Blues* on a record that accompanied his 1959 book *The Country Blues*. He also extolled Johnson's virtues and referred to Johnson's troubled life, and emotional difficulties. And in 1961, John Hammond, in his role as an executive producer at Columbia Records, arranged for the first full album of Robert Johnson recordings to be issued. Frank Driggs, a jazz enthusiast and scholar, produced the recording, and, in his liner notes, he too cast Robert in the role of the unfulfilled young genius, whose candle had burned out so quickly. The album was followed by a second reissue LP in 1970.

One of the things that made the Robert Johnson LP stand out was that, unlike many of the other blues reissues, such as Ma Rainey's recordings, the original recordings were surprisingly clean, and it was possible to understand most of the words. The record also made its way to England, where a young Eric Clapton and Keith Richards became devoted Robert Johnson fans. They marveled at the songs, and tried to learn the guitar parts. Meanwhile in the United States, Robert's legacy was carried on by John Hammond's son, himself a blues singer, and numerous other young white blues revivalists.

Despite all of this, Robert's audience at the time was still a relatively small cult following. However, in a few short years, the Rolling Stones recorded Robert's *Love in Vain*, and Eric Clapton, as a member of Cream, recorded *Crossroads*. These were million-selling records, but still most of the rock fans who bought them knew little or nothing about the life and music of Robert Johnson. In 1986, a movie called *Crossroads* appeared. In this movie one of the main characters was a blues harmonica player named Willie Brown, who sought redemption for making a deal with the devil at the cross-roads, where the devil gave Brown his musical talent in exchange for possession of his soul. Never mind that there was a real musician named Willie Brown, who had been a musical influence on Robert Johnson, in the mind of the mass audience, the movie was actually about Robert Johnson. Another contributing factor to this aspect of the legend was that ethnomusicologist David Evans had interviewed LeDell Johnson, brother of yet another (unrelated) Mississippi bluesman, Tommy Johnson, and LeDell stated that his brother had made a similar deal with Satan, trading his soul for musical talent.

Between the movie, the two men named Johnson, and off-hand statements by such blues men as Son House, who remarked that Johnson's improvement as a guitarist represented something super-natural, a certain segment of the blues audience became convinced that Robert literally had made a deal with the devil. Support for this view was given by Julio Finn's book *The Bluesman.* Finn was one of the few black scholars to write about the blues, and he saw white scholars' repudiation of the crossroads legend as a racist inability to acknowledge the power and influence of voodoo. To Finn the deal with the devil was something that literally happened, and he cited Haitian and African folkloristic sources as evidence that such a thing was possible.

This brings us to the final phase of Robert's posthumous career. In 1991, Columbia issued a double CD package that included every-thing that Robert Johnson ever recorded. Not only were all 29 songs on the CDs, there were also alternative takes. In many cases, Robert had recorded the same song twice. In listening to the CDs, we are able to construct some theories about how much of the music was improvised, and how much was presented in relatively formal, set musical arrangements. Three videos followed not long afterward, including a 1992 British TV documentary called *The Search for Robert Johnson*, in which John Hammond Jr. acted as a sort of trav-eling narrator, a 1997 documentary produced and directed by Peter Meyer titled *Can't You Hear the Wind Howl: The Life and Music of Robert Johnson*, and a 1999 documentary, *Hellhounds on My Trail: The Afterlife of Robert Johnson*, directed by Robert Mugge.

If this was not enough to feed the Robert Johnson media frenzy, Peter Guralnick's brief 1989 biography was followed in 2003 by the contentious *Robert Johnson: Lost and Found*, by Barry Lee Pearson and Bill McCulloch, and Elijah Wald's 2004 book, *Escaping the Delta: Robert Johnson and the Invention of the Blues*; more books are in the works. Blues fans have also long awaited blues researcher Mack McCormick's *Portrait of a Phantom*, some 30 years in the writing, and yet another book, this one by Steve LaVere. LaVere also wrote most of the notes for the Columbia double CD boxed set. LaVere is a controversial figure in the Johnson odyssey, because he owns the publishing rights to Johnson's songs, and has also acquired and copyrighted photographs of Johnson. Some blues scholars have attacked LaVere's interests as being essentially financially self-serving. All in all to date there have been four novels, two videos, a screenplay and a theater piece written about Robert Johnson.

The writers, videographers, blues scholars, and musicians who knew Robert seem to divide themselves into two camps. Julio Finn is probably the only one writing about Robert Johnson who takes the deal with the devil at the crossroads myth as literal truth. The other extreme is the position taken by Pearson and McCulloch, who seriously argue against the possibility of such a deal having ever occurred. Along the way they castigate virtually all previous blues scholars, such as Charters and Guralnick, for contributing to the lode of romantic fantasies that make up the legacy of Robert Johnson. Wald is more interested in trying to examine why these romantic fantasies exist, and is quick to acknowledge that most white blues fans or scholars came to their interest in blues because of the very romantic aspects of the music that appealed to them. For most it was a different culture, a different time, that inspired, and continues to inspire, people from all sorts of social, ethnic, and economic backgrounds far removed from the roots of the blues.

Gayle Dean Wardlow is the only one of these scholars who has lived in Mississippi for years, and he takes a calmer approach to the issues. He points out that the encounters of musicians, or others, with the devil have their roots in eighteenth-century New England. He adds that the notion of selling one's soul to the devil also appeared in literature in Washington Irving's 1824 story *The Devil and Tom Walker*, and again in Stephen Vincent Benet's *The Devil and Daniel Webster*, published in 1936. According to Steve LaVere,

Robert Johnson's probable teacher, Ike Zinneman, claimed to have learned to play guitar in a graveyard at midnight, sitting on tombstones. In country music, there is a periodical devoted to fiddle playing called *The Devil's Box*, and among deeply religious white southerners secular music has often been termed "the devil's music." Country-rock singer Charley Daniels even had a hit record called *The Devil in Georgia*, where a fiddler competes with the devil, defeating old Satan in a musical cutting session.

In 1983, a blues scholar named Michael Taft put together a computer search of blues subjects in his book *Blue Lyric Poetry: An Anthology*. Taft covered songs recorded from 1920 to 1942, and he transcribed over 2000 commercially recorded songs sung by over 350 singers. He turned up ten songs that included the word "devil" in their title; however, only one of these titles was a Robert Johnson song *Me and the Devil Blues*, with *Hell Hound on My Trail* occupying neighboring lyric territory. Taft omits the alternative title of Johnson's *Preaching Blues*, which is *Up Jumped the Devil*. As far as his songwriting went, Robert could hardly be accused of being unduly fixated on the devil as such, although the argument could be made that 3 titles out of a recorded repertoire of 29 songs represents a considerable portion of Johnson's total recorded work.

Possibly the best version of the last word belongs to blues scholar and surrealist Paul Garon. Garon wrote an entire book about a blues artist named Peetie Wheatstraw, who billed himself as "the devil's son-in-law." Garon writes,

> I am inclined to think that, as facts emerge and as the picture draws closer to completion, the romance, mystery and power that have always surrounded Peetie, his songs, and indeed the power of the blues as a whole, tend only to increase, while the subjects with which we deal are stripped of their vagaries and revealed in their own true light. For what stands then is often what could only have been dreamed of — and dreaming has always been our only hope.

Not a bad epitaph for Robert Johnson.

The recent books about Robert Johnson seem almost obsessed with tracing the various influences in his music. Elijah Wald does a detailed analysis of every one of Johnson's songs, mentioning such disparate influences as pianist Leroy Carr, guitarists Skip James, Lonnie Johnson, Kokomo Arnold, Tampa Red, Blind Boy Fuller, and Blind Willie McTell, as well as the vocal style of Peetie Wheatstraw, with his falsetto whoops. Undeniably Robert Johnson is a descendant of the Delta blues style, pioneered, as far as we know, by Charley Patton, and continued and developed by his disciples Son House and Willie Brown. The aspects of the Delta style that Robert certainly exemplifies include an intense guitar style, often including the use of a slide, a tortured high vocal style that crosses over into falsetto, and the use of the guitar as a second voice that essentially converses with the singer.

However, many of the influences that Wald notes seem farfetched at best. There is no reason to doubt that Johnson admired Lonnie Johnson, his unrelated namesake, but it is difficult to hear much musical influence in the two musicians' guitar styles. Robert sounds relatively crude and untutored compared with Lonnie's sophisticated jazz stylings. Although Robert undoubtedly played with some other musicians, they certainly did not include people such as Louis Armstrong, Duke Ellington, or Eddie Lang, all of whom Lonnie Johnson both played and recorded with. Furthermore, there is no evidence that Robert had mastered the harmonic complexities inherent in jazz guitar, which were very much a part of Lonnie's world. Given Robert's personality, it is hard to imagine him working in a normal band context.

Compared with the other Delta guitarists of the day, Robert had a greater grasp of the guitar's resources than Patton, House, or Willie Brown. He is more apt to use chords, and more modern chords than any of the others, and he avoids the heavy bass thumb slapping of Son House. He is closer in general to Charley Patton and Ishmon Bracey than to House, in the sense that many of his songs are medium tempo or faster. For the most part, he avoids the slow-tempo blues that House often favored, and also avoids single-note runs, except when he is playing with the slide. Bracey may well have been an influence, but Robert's playing is much more refined and structured than Bracey's work. I would say that of the Delta guitarists, Johnson's style is probably closest to Patton's, although not to the point where Patton seems to have been a major influence. Because we have no recordings of Johnson's mentor Ike

Zinneman, we have no notion of how much Ike's guitar style rubbed off on Johnson.

An interesting musical offshoot of the Johnson recordings is the tune *They're Red Hot*. This tune uses a ragtime chord progression common among Piedmont guitarists, and is by far the most playful of Johnson's recorded songs. It is indebted to the sort of performances that Blind Willie McTell or Pink Anderson commonly gave. However, Johnson's recording is not really an effective performance, and Robert does not seem as comfortable with the style as he was with Delta blues. Toward the end of the song he does not quite make the high vocal notes that he attempts on the recording. We can conjecture that this song came to him during his many travels, where he must have observed Piedmont guitar styles and songs.

The inevitable question is, what is it about Robert Johnson's music that has created such a furor among both blues fans, blues musicians, and even rock and rollers? First of all, Robert Johnson is a sufficiently capable guitarist that he requires no additional accompaniment. He is one of the few blues artists who never attempted to record with any other musicians. At his best Robert is able to keep the rhythm churning along with his right-hand fingers, and he utilizes the slide worn on his little finger to play lead lines, almost like horn lines. It is true, as Wald points out, that Kokomo Arnold was a more technically proficient slide guitarist than Robert was, and it is also true that Arnold played around with rhythmic subtleties, such as double time, in a way that Robert Johnson never did, at least on records. So why did Arnold not became a celebrated historical figure, with reissued records enjoying large-scale success?

One of Johnson's significant musical contributions was in adapting boogie woogie piano figures for the guitar. He was the first, or one of the first, blues musicians to do so.

Pearson and McCulloch might well attribute Johnson's success to the legend, even as they acknowledge that Robert was also a major-league talent. But there are also emotional elements in Robert's performances that have rarely been captured by other blues singers. Robert, like so many of his peers, may have recorded in a vain quest for fortune and fame, but there is a strong factor of credibility in his emotional performances. Another part of this credibility, as we will soon see, may have something to do with Robert's lyrics.

In some ways, the inclusion of multiple outtakes on the double CD box does not serve Robert Johnson particularly well. Part of the romantic image of the blues artist, like that of the jazz artist, is that these "untutored" (I am talking about image here, and not reality) musicians had an endless supply of original musical phrases at their command. Wald points out that Robert's recordings seemed to be set musical arrangements, as opposed to studio improvisations Hearing alternative takes of Robert Johnson's music, we can confirm that many of Robert's songs were indeed set pieces, with little variation from one performance of a song to another. Although the romantic blues fan may find this disappointing, Robert never intended for his music to appeal to an audience of middle-class intellectuals — not that he might not be quite pleased that his music is able to reach out to that audience as well. Perhaps we have overly stressed the improvisational element as a necessary component of all blues performances.

It is also necessary to acknowledge that as creative as some of the songs are, many of Johnson's guitar phrases are repeated countless times. Johnson was enormously fond of a blues turn around where he played, for example, a descending series of seventh chords, such as E7, Eb7, D7, or another figure where he played E major, followed by E7, A, and then E diminished seventh. Oddly the much more sophisticated guitarists Brownie McGhee and Josh White were also quite fond of these phrases. It is an oddly urban sound, juxtaposed with Robert's Delta blues techniques.

The lyrics of Robert's songs paint a picture that is not particularly a romantic one, unless your idea of a romantic figure includes someone with a seemingly endless and somewhat paranoid distrust of women. The image of women as duplicitous heartbreakers is a common one in blues lyrics, but Johnson seems to have had a particularly hard time, at least according to his songs. The heroine of *Kind Hearted Woman* breaks his heart when "she calls Mister So-and-So's name." In *I Believe I'll Dust My Broom*, Robert tells us his two-timing woman can "mistreat me, here, babe, but you can't when I get home." Song after song displays this same fundamental distrust of women. The woman in *Rambling on My Mind* treats him so unkindly that he leaves her in tears. Just when you think Robert is revealing a more emotionally vulnerable side of himself in *When You Got a Good Friend*, he warns the listener that it is often a close friend who hurts you the most. Other examples of Robert's warnings or complaints about unfaithful women include *Dead Shrimp Blues, If I Had Possession over Judgment Day, I'm a Steady Rollin' Man, From Four till Late,* and *Stop Breakin' down Blues.*

When Johnson is not complaining about low-down or treacherous women, he is usually feeling sorry for himself, most specifically in *Love in Vain,* where the singer follows his woman to the railroad station, tears in his eyes, while he watches her leave. Even in *Cross Road Blues,* the song that the "Robert-made-his-deal-with-the-devil" proponents think is the place where it all happened, he cries out to the Lord to save him, complains that he has no woman, and tells his friend delta guitarist Willie Brown, "I believe I'm sinkin' down."

Several other lyrics are versions of blues double entendres, where the apparent literal meaning of the lyric veils an obvious sexual reference. *Terraplane Blues* is one of the many blues that compares the functioning of a car engine to a woman's sexuality. This theme is found in many other blues, but the allusions in *Phonograph Blues* are a bit more common, including the stock line, "you made me love you, now your man have come," found in the blues standard *Easy Rider.* Even the lighter, almost raggy tune *They're Red Hot,* another double entendre tune, includes threats about just what the singer is going to do to his woman.

Several of Robert's songs are thinly veiled copies of other blues. *32-20 Blues* is a close copy of Skip James's *22-20.* In it, the singer goes back and forth between threatening his woman with his gun and his resentment at her running off with another man. *Milk Cow Calf Blues* is a close copy of Kokomo Arnold's *Milk Cow Blues.* However, we need to acknowledge that assigning originality is a dangerous game. In the case of *Milk Cow,* for example, Michael Taft prints two other lyrics with that song title; one dates from 1926, and is credited to Freddie Spruill, and the other is a 1930 recording by Sleepy John Estes. Both of these are considerably earlier than the 1934 Kokomo Arnold recording.

In the songs *Cross Road Blues, Stones in My Passway, If I Had Possession over Judgment Day, Preaching Blues (Up Jumped the Devil),* and *Hellhound on My Trail,* Robert is at his highest level of vocal and emotional intensity. It is these songs that give the listener the sense of invoking supernatural powers, and the singer's personal desperation. In *Hellhound,* the singer's woman has used black magic on him to keep him ramblin', and in *Passway* Robert claims that his "enemies have betrayed me." Finally, in *Me and the Devil Blues*, Robert has a short dialogue with Satan, who has literally knocked on his door. They leave the house together, and Robert declares that he will beat his woman until he is satisfied. It is up to the listener to determine whether it is the devil who has incited this violence, or whether Robert is claiming that it is his inner devils that are causing him to behave this way.

There are very few playful Robert Johnson songs, and not many where he reveals any attitude about women other than that they represent a vehicle for his needs and aggressions. In *Little Queen of Spades*, Robert finally relents; this song envisages a partnership where he and the gambling woman become partners, with her being the queen while he is the king, then "we can make our money green."

If we believe that an artist's songs are a window into his life experiences, examining Robert Johnson's lyrics brings to life a person who was a restless, dissatisfied wanderer, always seeking out the next woman, and seemingly never, or rarely, believing that she would offer anything more than temporary companionship and an outlet for the singer's sexual needs of the moment. Pearson and McCulloch would appear to be on safe ground in assuming that the so-called deal with the devil is simply a myth, fed by the romantic needs of blues fans, Robert's premature death, his seeming effect on other musicians and on listeners 60 and 70 years after his death, and the various anecdotes from his contemporaries about his disappearing at a moment's notice to continue his endless travels. The circumstances of his death were certainly also a contributing factor. The question remains: Without all of these circumstances coming into play, would Robert have simply become a forgotten blues singer, one of the many footnotes in the history of delta blues? And although Pearson and McCulloch seem to want to downplay the evident torment and intensity of Robert's vocal performances, one need not believe in the supernatural to react to these emotional vocal and instrumental performances.

There are so many other questions, ones that probably will never be answered. For example, was Robert in effect emotionally destroyed by the death of his first wife and child during the latter's birth? Did he relate to her in the same way that he subsequently treated, seemingly, all other women, or was it the circumstances of her death that made him cynical about human relationships? And, supernatural or not, how did Robert's guitar skills evolve? Was it the influence of Ike Zinneman or simply that Johnson was a sponge who traveled widely and absorbed all the musical styles that he heard during his travels. How much did he learn simply from listening to the recordings or performances of his contemporaries?

THE IMPACT OF ROBERT JOHNSON

The indisputable fact is that Robert Johnson has attained more popularity and achieved more staying power than any other blues singer of the twentieth century. His fans range from blues revivalists to rock and rollers, academics, researchers, and blues authors. His songs have been recorded by Eric Clapton and The Rolling Stones, and both Clapton and Keith Richards have paid tribute to Robert in their album notes for his CD reissues. Many of the British blues revivalists, such as Peter Green of the original Fleetwood Mac, Alexis Korner, and John Mayall, have paid tribute to him. Sixteen different artists performed Robert's songs on a 2001 CD, ranging from a few of Robert's remaining peers, including David "Honeyboy" Edwards and Robert Jr. Lockwood, to Gatemouth Brown, James Cotton, Taj Mahal, and some of the younger blues performers, including Susan Tedeschi and Butch Trucks. In 2004, Eric Clapton released *Me and Mr. Johnson,* a CD of his versions of Johnson's recordings.

Another level of influence that Robert had on the evolution of the blues was the work of his old traveling partner Johnny Shines, and, of course, the performances and recordings of Robert Jr. Lockwood. Elmore James literally added electricity to the bottleneck guitar style, and his recording of Robert's *Dust My Broom* not only became an R&B hit, but influenced many other musicians. Muddy Waters carried on the Robert Johnson legacy in the same sense that Robert had done with the works of Son House and Willie Brown, even though Muddy never knew Robert personally. None of these things could have been readily predicted at the time of Robert Johnson's death in 1938.

Seventy-five years after the death of Robert Johnson, his place in blues history seems more secure and significant than ever.

OTHER MISSISSIPPI ARTISTS

Tommy Johnson's recording career actually preceded that of Robert Johnson. He recorded from 1928 to 1930, and several of his songs, such as *Big Road Blues* and *Canned Heat Blues*, are popular among blues revival singers. David Evans, writing in his book *Big Road Blues*, points out that Tommy's blues were loosely structured, and probably changed from one performance to another. He makes this inference from his fieldwork recording of Tommy's brother, Mager. Johnson began playing guitar in Crystal Springs, Mississippi, and played with Son House, Willie Brown, and the less well-known Dick Bankston.

A set of bluesmen-songsters came from another delta town, Drew, Mississippi. A farm area with a majority black population, the area was home to many blues musicians. Chester (Howlin' Wolf) Burnett moved there at the age of 13. He later achieved notoriety as one of the fathers of the Chicago electric blues. Jackson was the home of the Chatmon family, a string band that performed in a variety of musical genres. Charley Patton's uncle was the patriarch of the family, and one of his sons, who recorded his solos under the name Bo Carter, specialized in double entendre risque songs, with a seemingly endless supply of sexual metaphors. The Mississippi Sheiks stringband featured several members of the Chatmon family. One younger family member, Sam Chatmon, was "rediscovered" in the 1970s and made several recordings over the next decades.

Booker (Bukka) White was born in 1906 in Houston, Mississippi, but as a teenager he spent time in Clarksdale, and supposedly met Charley Patton. He recorded both blues and gospel music in Memphis in 1930. White's blues compositions, which he called "sky songs" because he said they came to him from the sky, present an interesting and imaginative picture of his life and thoughts. His *Fixin' to Die* in particular presents a fascinating and intense view of family life, with the lines "I wouldn't mind dyin', but I can't stand to see my children cry." White was yet another musician who was rediscovered during the folk revival, and pursued a successful career playing at coffeehouses and at folk festivals.

Skip James, from Bentonia, Mississippi, had one of the more unusual and even eccentric lives of all the Mississippi bluesmen. Skip was a preacher, a bootlegger, and a bordello piano player.

He was spotted by talent scout and furniture store owner H.C. Speir, and sent to Grafton, Wisconsin, to record for Paramount Records in 1930. James was never paid for his unsuccessful recordings, and he retired from performing blues music. He later started a gospel group in Dallas, Texas, and became an ordained minister, but in 1964, he was convinced to resume playing the blues. He appeared at the Newport Folk Festival, and continued to perform until his death 5 years later. James was one of the few bluesmen who played both guitar and piano. James had a high tenor voice, and his voice is readily distinguishable from that of any other singer.

PIEDMONT AND OTHER REGIONAL STYLES

The Piedmont region of the Carolinas spawned a different style of blues from that of the Delta. Perhaps because life was easier in the southeast for blacks than on the oppressive plantations of the Delta, the blues had a more light-hearted, ragtime-influenced sound in this region. The Piedmont and related performers were more firmly in the tradition of the songster — performing a wide range of popular material — than the more hardcore Delta blues musicians.

Blind Boy Fuller was a blues artist from Durham, North Carolina. He recorded prolifically, often using harmonica player Sonny Terry on his recordings, along with Bull City Red, a washboard player. On some of his recordings he also used Blind Gary Davis as a second guitarist. (Davis, an excellent ragtime guitarist who later performed as Rev. Gary Davis, became a major star in the blues revival of the 1950s and 1960s.) Some of his tunes, such as *Rag Mama Rag* and *Trucking My Blues Away*, were re-recorded by white folk and blues artists in the 1960s. Fuller died in 1941, but his recordings remained quite influential for years after his death. Brownie McGhee, whom we will discuss in more detail in Chapter 5, recorded under the name Blind Boy Fuller #2, even writing and recording a Fuller tribute called *The Death of Blind Boy Fuller*.

Buddy Moss was a contemporary of Blind Boy Fuller. He started out as a harmonica player, but became a fine guitarist on his way to a successful career when a 6-year jail term interrupted his work. Moss was rediscovered during the late 1960s, and although he did record, the folk revival did not embrace him in the same way that it lionized Brownie McGhee and Sonny Terry.

Josh White was born in Greenville, South Carolina, and began recording in 1933, when he was only 19 years old. His early recordings were lighthearted blues, showing off his fine guitar playing and pleasant voice. However, most of White's fame was in the role of a cabaret and concert singer, based in New York City, beginning in the 1940s. He became a major star in the United States and Europe during the first folk revival of the 1950s (see Chapter 5).

Tampa Red (Hudson Whitaker) was a Piedmont-born musician who ended up living in Chicago. He recorded hundreds of sides, in duet with Georgia Tom (Thomas A. Dorsey) and with a variety of other musicians. Tampa played slide guitar, but not in the intense Mississippi style; rather he specialized in pure and sweet single-note playing. His many songs varied from straight blues to ragtime-influenced party songs, many of them with double entendres, such as *Let Me Play With Your Poodle*. Tampa had a light and airy voice, much like his guitar style. His house in Chicago was headquarters for many blues singers, and he recorded from 1928 well into the 1940s, producing one last recording for Prestige during the folk-blues revival in the 1960s. Although most of Tampa's songs were blues, his hokum tunes crossover into the songster category.

Atlanta, Georgia, was one of the central areas where songsters seem to have congregated. One of the most interesting of these artists was Blind Willie McTell. McTell's recording career lasted from 1927 until 1959, although it was an episodic rather than a continuous career. Willie was one of several Atlanta artists who played twelve-string guitar, a fairly unusual instrument for the blues. On the twelve string, all six strings are paired, with the second string tuned an octave lower than the primary one. It requires quite a bit of strength to finger it in the left hand, and it is difficult to play cleanly. McTell did not strum the twelve string, unlike most of his contemporaries, but rather fingerpicked it. His repertoire varied from blues to religious songs, and ragtime-vaudeville-influenced tunes such as the *Atlanta Strut* and a recitation with guitar accompaniment, the *Dyin' Crapshooter's Blues*. Another of McTell's songs, *Talkin' to Myself*, even finds him scat-singing. His *Statesboro Blues* was one of the most interesting of Willie's compositions, and it was covered decades after McTell's death by the Allman Brothers Band, who scored a major hit with it.

Barbecue Bob (Robert Hicks) was another Atlanta songster who played twelve string, and was first recorded by Columbia A&R man Frank Walker in 1927. Hicks' success also led to a recording deal for his brother Charlie, and over the years Bob recorded 62 sides. Barbecue Bob's twelve-string guitar technique utilizes strumming rather than McTell's more subtle fingerpicking. Bob's songs varied from blues to ragtime-influenced tunes. Bob also recorded in a trio with guitarist Curley Weaver and harmonica and guitar player Buddy Moss, where he played twelve string with a slide. Bob recorded a couple of recitations with his brother Charlie under the titles *It Won't be Long Now — Part 1* and *Part 2*. On these songs, the brothers joke amiably about their women leaving them, and boast of how they never run out of women.

Another popular Piedmont-styled guitarist was Blind Blake (Arthur Phelps). Blake was born in Jacksonville, and had an extensive recording career, cutting 82 solo sides for Paramount Records in 1926–1932. He also accompanied numerous blues singers. Blake was noted for his fast and accurate finger picking, and although his singing is perfectly adequate, it is always secondary to his playing. He recorded a number of guitar solos with spoken interjections. Some of these are blues, some show a ragtime influence, and some even cross over to boogie-woogie. Unlike most of the other Piedmont artists, Blake migrated to Chicago. He disappeared after his last recording session in 1932, and it is not known what happened to him. Some of the other artists whose records he played on include Ma Rainey and Gus Cannon, and he is one of a very small group of musicians whom Rev. Gary Davis acknowledged as peers.

LEADBELLY AND LONNIE JOHNSON

Huddie (Leadbelly) Ledbetter gained fame late in life as a folksinger, but he was a native of Louisiana, born about 30 miles from Shreveport in 1888. Although he was best known for playing twelve-string guitar, Leadbelly also played concertina and six-string guitar, and even a little piano. Leadbelly was discovered by John and Alan Lomax while serving a prison term in Louisiana. After his release from prison, he traveled with the Lomaxes and learned songs from other singers, wherever the Lomax collecting excursions took him. Lomax helped Leadbelly get his first record deals, and later he became the darling of various New York folksingers and fans, including Woody Guthrie and Pete Seeger. Leadbelly developed a unique form of song-stories where he would utilize extensive spoken introductions to his songs. These narratives were sometimes virtually as long as the songs themselves. Another characteristic of Leadbelly's music was that he began many songs on the I7 chord, A7, for example, in the key of A. This gave his songs a unique and very recognizable sound. Leadbelly died in 1949, just as the folk revival was beginning; 6 months after his death, The Weavers (featuring a young Pete Seeger) had a major pop hit with *Irene, Goodnight*, a song they learned from Leadbelly. We will discuss Leadbelly's famous protest song, *The Bourgeois Blues*, later in the book (see Chapter 5).

Lonnie Johnson was a musician absolutely beyond category. Born in New Orleans in 1899, Johnson's recordings and career spanned an accompanying role for singers, notably Texas Alexander, playing jazz guitar with Louis Armstrong's Hot Seven, to blues-jazz duets with white guitarist Eddie Lang, guitar solos, a recording session with Duke Ellington, a rhythm and blues hit in 1947 for King records, a sabbatical from the music business until the late 1950s, and rediscovery and another string of recordings and successful European tours during the blues revival. Johnson sang and played everything from pop standards to blues to jazz, and he was enormously influential on many other blues musicians, including Robert Johnson and B.B. King. Elvis Prestey and Jerry Lee Lewis even recorded their own version of Johnson's R&B hit *Tomorrow Night*. Johnson had a superb guitar technique, best heard on the reissues of his brilliant duets with Eddie Lang. His singing was relaxed and somewhat restrained compared with many of the more country-blues artists.

MR. CHARLEY'S BLUES: WHITE BLUES PERFORMERS

Piedmont blues, and the work of the songsters in general, involved quite a lot of music that showed similarities to the white vaudeville and country music traditions. There are many songs that have been collected by folklorists that seem to have originated in the minstrel era, and that were passed back into tradition, and learned by black musicians. These include songs, fiddle tunes, recitations, and even spoken interjections that are frequently found on blues records. At the same time there were a number of country artists who recorded blues or, like Jimmie Rodgers, used elements of the blues in their performances and recordings. Rodgers and Western Swing band-leader Bob Wills were probably the most famous white singers who sang blues, or who used blues lyrics in their songs. Rodgers recorded a series of songs that included yodeling, which blues scholar Tony Russell speculates may have been Rodger's interpreta-tion of the falsetto singing found in some traditional blues performances. Besides Wills, other country-swing artists such as Milton Brown and Al Dexter often performed blues. It is also worth noting that many of the biggest country stars, including Hank Williams Sr., Bill Monroe, and influential guitarist Merle Travis, have mentioned in interviews that they were strongly influenced by black musicians in their formative musical years. Many other country musicians do not display an obvious blues influence in their music, but their repertoire draws from a sort of common well that exists in black and white music. Examples include the ballads *John Henry*, *Casey Jones*, *Frankie and Johnny*, also called *Frankie and Albert*, and the bad man ballad *Railroad Bill*. Minstrel tunes such as *Old Dan Tucker* or *The Boatmen Dance* are also found in both racial groups.

Country guitarists Frank Hutchison and Sam McGee may have been the white performers who best absorbed blues guitar tech-niques. Both of them were fingerpickers, and Hutchison also used a knife to play slide guitar. Hutchison recorded in the late 1920s and is best known for his blues-like song, *The Train That Carried My Girl from Town*. He acknowledged learning guitar from two black musicians whom he knew in his native West Virginia. Hutchison's guitar sounds exciting and authentic, but his vocals sound some-what thin, a pattern that persisted in many blues performances by white musicians during the folk music revival of the 1960s. Another early recording artist, Jimmy Tarlton, who recorded with Tom Darby, played slide guitar in a blues fashion, and Darby sang blues songs, combining blues vocal slides with yodeling.

Folk music scholar Alan Lomax characterized vocal styles as being executed with an open or a closed throat. The open-throat style of singing is characteristically African, and the closed-throat, more pinched style of singing is typical of most country singing. This is most noticeable if we compare delta blues styles with country artists who sing the blues. The Piedmont style does not use as much open-throat singing, and is kind of half-way between the two methods of vocal production.

There are several reissue CDs that include performances of "white blues." The Columbia double CD package *White Country Blues 1926–1938: A Lighter Shade of Pale* is an excellent resource for listening to performances by white blues singers. Riley Puckett's so-called *A Darkie's Wail* is essentially the song *John Henry* played as an instrumental on slide guitar. A number of the songs on these recordings use the word "blues" in their titles and include the use of the flatted third and or seventh notes, but are not in traditional blues format with its repeated lyric lines. *The Yodel Blues, Part I* and *II* is a particularly odd feature of this reissue. The artists are two Mexican Americans, Val and Pete Martinez, recording in 1928. The tune is very much indebted to Jimmie Rodgers, and includes yodeling and slide guitar playing. There is even a white guitarist-singer named Larry Hensley who attempts to imitate Blind Lemon Jefferson, singing his *Match Box Blues*. The instrumental work is quite convincing, and the vocal is closer to black vocal styles than most of the other cuts by world-be white blues singers. Last but not least, this CD package features two cuts by the Allen Brothers, singing and playing tenor banjo and kazoo. When these records were first issued, Columbia actually released them in their "race" record series, supposedly prompting a lawsuit by the insulted white artists.

Given the racist climate of the south, one might well wonder why white artists would want to sing blues in the first place. Tony Russell, writing in his pioneering study *Blacks, Whites and Blues*, theorizes that white artists found blues styles liberating, because it freed them from the clichés of country music. As he puts it, "there are no little whitewashed cabins in the world of the blues, no grey-haired mothers, no churches in the wildwood," all images typically found in country songs. He sees the blues as allowing the white artist to delve into areas not permitted in traditional country music. It is also clear, I believe, that many of the artists liked this music, and respected its creators.

HOLY BLUES

Holy blues are songs with religious lyrics that are in a blues format, often, although not always, featuring blues guitar accompaniments. There were blues artists such as Charley Patton, Blind Lemon Jefferson, and Josh White who made recordings in this style, but there were two artists who dominated the idiom: Blind Willie Johnson and Rev. Gary Davis. Johnson created an amazing musical tapestry with his intense slide guitar playing, and his gruff, powerful voice. Johnson was a Texas street preacher who performed on the streets of Dallas. He recorded initially as a solo artist, and later with his wife Angeline. He recorded for Columbia between 1927 and 1930. His most dramatic recording was the song *Dark Was the Night*, which includes a guitar solo accompanied by Johnson's low-voiced humming. Bob Dylan, Eric Clapton, and Ry Cooder are among the contemporary artists who have covered Johnson's music.

Gary Davis was originally a blues guitarist who appeared on some of Blind Boy Fuller's 1930s recordings, but in 1937, he became an ordained minister, and thereafter was reluctant to play blues in public. During the early 1940s he moved to New York, and during the 1950s he became an enormously influential figure, teaching guitar to many young white New York blues revivalists, including Stefan Grossman and Jorma Kaukonen (later a founding member of the Jefferson Airplane and Hot Tuna). On Tuesday nights Gary played at Tiny Ledbetter's apartment on the lower east side in New York City, a gathering spot for blues revivalists. Dozens of young guitarists were heavily influenced by Davis, whether or not they actually took guitar lessons from him. Davis's repertoire included ragtime piano pieces, Sousa marches, and turn-of-the-century parlor tunes, as well as blues and gospel songs. Davis had a sort of unique bounce to his guitar work, and his gruff, impassioned singing was highly emotional. Although the bulk of his recorded work consisted of religious songs, his autobiographical *Lord, I Wish I Could See* is a rare glimpse into his life and everyday life.

THE ROLE OF INDIVIDUAL INSTRUMENTS

The dominant instrument of the folk blues was the guitar, but certainly piano and harmonica were cast in fairly prominent roles.

Instruments such as the fiddle and banjo were present to a lesser degree.

The Piedmont and Delta guitar styles are quite different. The Piedmont guitarists' music is:

- ragtime-influenced
- chord-based (full chords are played and various chord progressions are utilized)
- lightly textured, for example, if a slide or knife was used, it was to play sweet-toned single notes, not chords

The Piedmont guitarists utilized fingerpicking styles in the right hand somewhat similar to those of white artists of the period. If there was harmonica accompaniment, it tended to be melodic, not rhythmic. Piedmont jug bands performed in related musical styles, but added other instruments

The Delta styles featured:

- stinging, intense guitar styles.
- a slide or knife used to increase intensity, in other words rhythmically rather than melodically.
- open tunings (tuning the guitar to an open chord rather than the standard guitar tuning of EADGBE). The two most popular tunings were the G (chord) tunings, using the notes DGDGBD, and the D tuning, with the guitar tuned to DADF#AD. Some of the delta players also tuned to E, A, or E minor chords.
- a tendency to stick to I–IV–V chord progressions.
- a song structure that is somewhat freer and less oriented around twelve-bar formulas.

Delta guitarists often play entire songs without the use of full chords; the guitar may double the vocal melody, or play harmony to it. The right thumb often pounds the strings aggressively. The guitar is used to convey emotion, and playing techniques, such as those used by Son House, are often rougher and cruder than Piedmont styles. When the electric guitar became popular, and bending guitar strings became a characteristic gesture, guitarists such as Albert King would tune the guitar below its normal pitch, because it made the strings easier to bend.

These are broad generalizations, and should only be taken as a point of departure. They are not intended to be absolute statements.

The Texas guitarists used elements of both styles. To generalize, they were rougher than Piedmont styles, but less intense than the Delta techniques. Some guitarists, including Bukka White, used the guitar to imitate environmental sounds, typically trains.

The piano was necessarily more of an urban phenomenon, because it is not a portable instrument. Some of the blues pianists recording during the 1920s and 1930s include Leroy Carr, also a composer and singer, Roosevelt Sykes, Jesse James, Pinetop Smith, Speckled Red Joshua Altheimer, Cow Cow Davenport, Little Brother Montgomery, and Peetie Wheatstraw. Carr was tremendously popular, thanks to his relaxed vocal style that was more modern sounding than some of the other traditional blues singers. He was often accompanied on record by guitarist "Scrapper" Blackwell, who played distinctive single-string riffs, also a more modern style than used by the earlier blues guitarists.

Some musical characteristics of blues piano are:

- Tremolos between the third and flatted third of a chord (E flat to E on a C chord).
- Dotted eighth notes followed by a sixteenth note in the left hand (long note–short note, long note–short note, etc.).
- Using the bass line to answer the vocal.
- The left hand keeps a steady rhythm, while the right hand plays ad lib musical fills.
- Use of boogie woogie bass lines, for example, on a C chord C–E–G–A–C–A–G–E, followed by the same intervals on the IV and V chords of the key (F and G in the key of C).
- Omitting the third of the chord. In a C chord, this would be the E (C–E–G). By omitting the E note, the player avoids the issue of the blue note (the E flat). The chord might be played simply with the two notes C and G, or by doubling the C an octave higher, giving the notes C–G–C.

There were also pianists who essentially accompanied guitarists, rather than playing lead parts. T.A. Dorsey, who often accompanied Tampa Red and pianists Joshua Altheimer and later Blind John Davis, are examples of piano-accompanists.

Harmonica was most typically found in jug bands, or as accompaniment for guitarists. There were a few of the harmonica players, including Noah Lewis or Sonny Terry, who were capable of performing solos on this modest instrument. Typical devices included imitating trains or fox chases, growling through the reeds of the harmonica, or imitating natural sounds. Both Sonny Terry and white harmonica artist Salty Holmes did feature pieces where they imitated a baby saying "I want my mama." Later harmonica artists, notably Little Walter, played chromatic harmonica, enabling them to play sharps and flats, or utilized as many as four harmonicas on the same tune, enabling them to play notes not readily available on a single harmonica. Later the Chicago blues players also amplified the harmonica, which allowed them to play musical parts equivalent to what horn players could do. These parts were single-note melodies, instead of chordal or rhythmic punctuations.

Other instruments that were used on folk blues records include the five- and six-string banjos, the tenor (four-string) banjo, the mandolin, and the violin. The six-string banjo is tuned exactly like a guitar, so it could be used interchangeably with that instrument. Jugs bands also used such homemade instruments as jugs, combs, and washboards. The banjo and mandolin could be played in a melodic style, or as rhythmic instruments, chugging the chords. There are also some examples of banjo playing that utilize a knife or slide, including the recordings of white banjoist Doc Walsh.

MEMPHIS MINNIE: WOMEN AND THE FOLK BLUES

There were relatively few women folk blues artists. The typical folk blues artist was a singing guitarist who traveled from town to town by hitchhiking or by riding freight trains. Few women during this period would have the interest or courage to pursue this lifestyle. Although there are a few recordings of some outstanding women folk blues artists, such as Geechie Wiley, Memphis Minnie is the only woman folk blues artist who became famous.

Minnie's real name was Minnie Douglas, and her recording career spanned three decades, starting in 1929. Her records generally feature two guitars. Minnie always played lead guitar, and first Kansas Joe (Joe McCoy) and later Little Son Joe played rhythm. Minnie was married to each of them in turn. On some of her records Joe's brother, Charlie (McCoy), plays mandolin, and her later recordings featured richer instrumentation, including piano, bass, and occasionally drums. Not only was Minnie an excellent guitarist, who reputedly defeated Big Bill Broonzy in a guitar contest, but she was also an excellent songwriter. Her songs *Me and My Chauffeur Blues* was recorded by Jefferson Airplane, and the songs *What's the Matter With the Mill?* and *Bumble Bee Blues* were also recorded or rewritten and copied by various other blues artists.

Summary

The heyday of the folk blues was the period 1920–1930. The three primary styles where the dark and intense blues from the Mississippi Delta, the ragtime-flavored and lighter textured Piedmont Blues from the Carolinas and Georgia, and the Texas blues, which were midway between the powerful Delta and more relaxed Piedmont styles. The most famous performers were Blind Lemon Jefferson out of Texas, Charley Patton and Robert Johnson from the Mississippi Delta, and Blind Willie McTell and Blind Blake in the ragtime-influenced Piedmont style. Other musical influences during this period included jug band music, holy blues, and white country adaptations of the blues. As time went on, artists were themselves influenced by recordings, and they began to combine different elements of these various genres.

4

RHYTHM AND BLUES
AND THE BEGINNING
OF ELECTRIC BLUES:
1940–1960

TIMELINE: 1940–1960

1941	United States entered World War II after Japanese attack on Pearl Harbor
	Alan Lomax recorded Muddy Waters for Library of Congress
1945	World War II ends
1946	T-Bone Walker recorded *Call It Stormy Monday* with electric guitar
1947	Muddy Waters made his first recordings in Chicago
1949	Long-playing (LP) record introduced
1950	Korean war began
1952	B.B. King had first major R&B hit, *Three O'Clock Blues*
1953	Bill Haley's first recording released (*Crazy, Man Crazy*)
1954	Elvis Presley and Ray Charles hit the charts
1955	Rosa Parks refused to give up her bus seat to a white person in Montgomery, Alabama. Black bus boycott began.
1956	Russians crushed Hungarian uprising
1960	John F. Kennedy elected U.S. president

In this chapter, we will trace the many threads that came together from the early 1940s through 1960 in black popular music to influence the growth of the blues. We will begin in Chicago, to where many blacks emigrated from the Mississippi Delta during the

Depression, in search of employment and better living standards. We will then look at the post-World War II rise of rhythm and blues (R&B), and the many small record labels that helped foster its popularity. We will profile three electric blues stars who enjoyed initial success in the R&B charts, John Lee Hooker, B.B. King, and Muddy Waters. We will look at several regional blues scenes in the 1950s, beginning again with Chicago, then moving to Los Angeles, New York, and New Orleans. Finally, we will look at how early rock was influenced by blues and R&B music.

CHICAGO BLUES: 1935–1950

Chicago was a center of blues performance from the mid-1930s on, although today when we say "Chicago Blues," we are usually referring to the small-combo, electric blues performed from the late 1940s in many Southside Chicago clubs. In fact, Chicago musicians did much to preserve and extend the Delta blues traditions that began with Charlie Patton and Robert Johnson. In his book *Chicago Breakdown*, Mike Rowe points out that from 1930 to 1950 more than 60 percent of the Black migrants to Chicago came from Mississippi (136,960 out of a total of 228,715 people). Rowe contrasts these numbers with the Texas-dominated migration to California, and the largely southeastern state exodus to New York. It is not surprising, then, that Chicago was so heavily influenced by the Delta blues style.

The easiest way to view the transformation of the Chicago blues is through the musical evolution of recordings by Big Bill Broonzy and Tampa Red. Both of these artists were known as the sort of influential leaders on the blues recording scene who not only recorded and wrote their own songs, but also organized sessions and rehearsals for other artists. Tampa's house was a sort of blues central headquarters, with two pianos, ongoing informal blues sessions, and a casual booking agency for jobs. Tampa was born in Georgia, but Broonzy was a native of Mississippi. Both artists started recording in 1928. Their early recordings are either solo works, or include only one or two accompanying instruments. Both musicians ended up in Chicago during the 1930s, where they found good opportunities to perform and record. Over the course of the 1930s, both of them began to include additional instrumentalists.

Broonzy's late 1930s works include the *Memphis Five*, with an instrumentation of piano, alto sax, string bass, and trumpet. Other Broonzy records from the late 1930s include clarinet, and by 1940 drums appear. The saxophone is particularly notable because it presages the rhythm and blues sound of the late 1940s and 1950s. The trumpet and clarinet parts are somewhat reminiscent of Dixieland jazz playing. In many cases, the guitar is dominated by the piano, and reduced to a secondary role. However, it is important to remember that all recording at this time required musicians to play live with no overdubs; the presence of an excellent piano player such as Joshua Altheimer enabled Broonzy to relax and concentrate on his vocals.

Tampa Red's work evolved in a similar way. Initially, he recorded alone or in partnership with pianist Georgia Tom (Dorsey). By 1936, Tampa played guitar and kazoo, and his band included a clarinet, piano, string bass, and an additional guitarist. On recordings made a year later, the horns include tenor sax and trumpet, piano is retained, and a drummer is added to the proceedings. (According to pianist John Davis, quoted in the album notes to the CD reissue, *Tampa Red: The Bluebird Recordings, 1936–1938*, the use of the horns was the idea of record producer-entrepreneur Lester Melrose. Melrose oversaw many Chicago recordings in the 1930s by black artists.) Although Broonzy pretty much stayed with blues, many of Tampa's recordings from the late 1930s sound as much pop as blues. The standard 16-bar blues songs with lyric repeats have been abandoned, and the structure and the subject matter of the recordings are close to pop music.

One of the interesting things about the Chicago blues of the 1940s and early 1950s (before the electric guitar and drums became a prominent part of the sound) was that, although Chicago was the home of numerous people born in Mississippi, the so-called *Bluebird Beat* (named for the record label on which many of these artists appeared) that was popularized by Broonzy and Tampa Red was not a Delta sound at all, but a sort of revved up and laundered version of the Piedmont blues. In the same way, the two most influential Chicago-based artists of the earlier period were Piedmont artist Blind Blake and Texas-songster Blind Lemon Jefferson

Another influential artist in the evolution of the Chicago blues scene was John Lee Curtis (Sonny Boy) Williamson. (In homage to

Williamson, another musician, Rice Miller, borrowed Sonny Boy's name, and the second Sonny Boy also had a successful recording career; Miller is often known in the literature as "Sonny Boy Williamson #2" to avoid confusion.) The original Sonny Boy was born in Jackson, Tennessee, but spent quite a bit of time at his uncle's house in St. Louis. Sonny Boy was one of a number of St. Louis musicians who migrated to Chicago. St. Louis had its own blues scene, and it served as kind of a way station between Memphis and Chicago. Sonny Boy was a songwriter, vocalist, and harmonica ace who recorded over 120 sides for Bluebird. Sonny Boy's recordings featured a small combo, almost more like a string band than the sort of jump blues that Broonzy and Tampa were performing. The instrumentation was piano, an additional guitar, and mandolin. The harmonica generally functions as the lead instrument, and the sound was later to be further developed by Little Walter in the early 1950s. Although the harmonica was not yet amplified, Sonny Boy plays lead lines that foreshadow the use of the instrument for solo instrumental lines, resembling what a saxophone ordinarily would play.

Roosevelt Sykes was a piano player whose recorded work evolved in a similar fashion to that of Big Bill Broonzy. Sykes was born in 1906 in Elar, Arkansas, and his lengthy recording career continued into the late 1970s. Many of his early recordings, starting in 1929, were either his own piano/vocal solos, or songs where he accompanied a singer on piano. However, by 1941, he was recording with a bass player, guitarist, and drummer. Another popular pianist, Big Maceo (Maceo Merriweather), did not make it in the recording studio until 1941. Maceo was born in Georgia in 1905, and moved north to Detroit in 1926. Maceo's first recordings were organized by the omnipresent Lester Melrose in Chicago. In these sessions, Maceo accompanied Tampa Red, as well as making other recordings where Maceo was the soloist.

As the black population moved north, there was a definite decline in interest in the older country blues. In the urban barroom atmosphere, a combo provided musicians a better chance to be heard. Bass players and drummers also provided a more regular rhythmic pulse, which was a definite improvement from the point of view of a dancer. The earlier country blues singers had played outdoors and in small southern juke joints, and no one had particularly noticed their more casual approach to keeping time. Although the continuing flow of delta migrants to Chicago offered the blues musician a definite audience for blues, as time moved on and the black population was exposed to jazz, and later to rhythm and blues, it began to lose interest in the older blues styles. These black emigrants identified the blues with their hard life in the south, replete with poverty and sharecropping. This music and its associations became less and less attractive to the urbanized population. Out of this restlessness with the down-home subject matter and rural instrumentation of the folk blues artists came the impetus for rhythm and blues.

RHYTHM AND BLUES

When recording companies began issuing records by African Americans aimed at an African American market, they established special catalogs — and sometimes separate labels — to present this music. Searching for a name for this music, the labels originally referred to African American music records as "race" records. Race originally referred to "the race," a term often used by black writers and journalists in the earlier decades of the twentieth century. By the end of World War II, the term had become dated, and some felt it had negative connotations. In 1949, Jerry Wexler, an editor at *Billboard* — the leading trade journal for the music business — who later went on to a distinguished career as a record producer at Atlantic Records, substituted the term "rhythm and blues" (often shortened to "R&B") for the word "race." No one seems to know where the term rhythm and blues actually came from, but throughout the 1950s and into the 1960s it became the designated term for black popular music recorded by, and mostly marketed to, African Americans.

THE BLUES GO ELECTRIC: T-BONE WALKER

Rhythm and blues was characterized by a new sound: the sound of the electric guitar. Along with the honking saxophone, piano, bass, and drums, the guitar became a leading voice in every R&B ensemble. Amplification made this possible.

Before the introduction of the electric guitar, the guitar was not really an efficient instrument for playing solo lines with orchestral groups or even small ensembles. During the 1930s, larger instruments, featuring arched tops and F holes, were introduced for use in jazz bands, and they were adequate for playing rhythm parts, where the guitarist used a flat pick and played chords. Playing melodic lines required the use of microphones, and even with a microphone the guitar tended to be drowned out by horns. Eddie Lang and Lonnie Johnson had pioneered the technique of playing single-string lines on the guitar during the late 1920s and into the 1930s in band settings, but often a large section of the band had to "drop out" on recordings in order for these guitarists to be heard. Many blues guitarists used guitars with a resonator and a metal body. A popular instrument was made by the National guitar company, and so these instruments are often referred to as "National Steels." These guitars indeed were louder than the earlier wood-bodied guitars, and they were particularly useful for playing with a bottleneck slide. But even resonator guitars did not cut through the sound of several horns and a drum set.

During the 1930s, several guitarists experimented with electric guitars. Among the earliest of these musicians were Les Paul, Eddie Durham, and Floyd Smith. By 1939, Charlie Christian was playing the electric guitar, and he was the first outstanding jazzman to do so. T-Bone Walker was a Dallas musician who was a friend of Christian's, and inevitably, he also picked up the electrified instrument. Walker was a guitarist who also had sung with big bands, so the electric instrument fit him perfectly. In 1947 he recorded *Call It Stormy Monday (But Tuesday Is Just as Bad)*. Walker also wrote this tune, which became a blues standard.

Walker's influence extended beyond the simple use of the electric guitar and the writing of this song. T-Bone was the first one to use the guitar to play melodic phrases like a horn. He also utilized the guitar to answer his vocals. Many other blues musicians had done this in the past, but not with band accompaniment. Because Walker had basically cut his musical teeth playing jazz, it was natural that his recordings had one foot in jazz, and the other in blues. Walker was also a showman who played the guitar behind his back and was renowned for his dancing skills. Despite all this, T-Bone had a genuine folk blues background, and as a young boy he had been a lead boy for Blind Lemon Jefferson on the streets of Dallas. He also grew up playing banjo, mandolin, violin, and ukulele.

T-Bone Walker influenced many other guitarists, the most important of whom was B.B. King. B.B. mirrored Walker's single electric lines, and also used horn players in his combo. Whereas Walker lived during a time when the blues became passé to black audiences, B.B. has a huge audience of both blacks and whites, and continues to perform widely today.

MUDDY WATERS AND THE CHICAGO DELTA SOUND

Muddy Waters grew up on Stovall's plantation in the Delta, the same place that Charley Patton had lived. Muddy's real name was McKinley Morganfield, and he was "discovered" by folklorist Alan Lomax in 1941. On this trip, Lomax was accompanied by black musician-composer John W. Work, who later published song collections of his own. Muddy recorded for Lomax both as a soloist and with violinist Son Sims. This opportunity to hear himself recorded, albeit on semiprofessional gear, stimulated Muddy's desire to leave Mississippi behind and go up north.

Muddy headed for Chicago in 1943, where he was befriended by Big Bill Broonzy. Initially he played in the bottleneck style that he had heard utilized by Son House, and occasionally by Robert Johnson. In Chicago, he learned from guitarist Blue Smitty (Claude Smith) to play without the bottleneck. He played with Sonny Boy Williamson for 8 months, and he recorded some unreleased sides with the ubiquitous Lester Melrose. Muddy formed a band with guitarist Jimmy Rogers, a drummer, and after some false starts, dynamic harmonica wizard Little Walter. In 1947, Muddy made his first records for Chicago independent label Chess Records. He even re-recorded for Chess some of the songs that he had recorded for Lomax, but by this time he was playing amplified guitar.

It is difficult to overestimate the influence of Muddy Waters on the evolution of the blues. A number of Muddy's recordings became rhythm and blues hits. Some of them were his re-workings of songs that he heard from other delta musicians, some were his own songs, and later on he recorded quite a few songs by Chess Records' session leader-contractor-bass man Willie Dixon. But it was not simply Muddy's records that were important. Jim Rooney in his book *Bossmen* describes Muddy as a major twentieth-century musician because of all of the other important musicians who passed through his band. In Muddy's case, Little Walter became almost the ultimate harmonica soloist, playing amplified harp like a saxophone, and later recording several giant hit records on his own. Others who passed through Waters' band included harmonica players Junior Wells, Carey Bell, and James Cotton, guitarists Pat Hare, Buddy Guy, and Jimmy Rodgers, and pianists Otis Spann and Pinetop Perkins. Almost all of these musicians went on to form their own bands, and recorded albums under their own names.

But Muddy's influence was not limited to black blues musicians. He also profoundly influenced such white Chicago bluesmen as Elvin Bishop, Michael Bloomfield, and Paul Butterfield. He even recorded with some of them during the white blues revival of the 1960s and 1970s. Muddy toured widely in Europe and all over the United States. The English rock band The Rolling Stones actually took their name from a line in one of Muddy's songs, "Gonna be a rollin' stone" from *Rollin' Stone*. Many of the English rock groups recorded Muddy's songs, or the Willie Dixon tunes that he had recorded.

But possibly Muddy's greatest contribution was that he retained many of the original folk blues elements in his recordings and performances. These included:

- Slide guitar playing
- Songs written in traditional blues form
- Soulful and direct vocal performances

Possibly more than any single individual, Muddy Waters influenced the direction of the blues. By adding electricity to the guitar and harmonica, and by using a drummer, Muddy's music was lively and danceable, and adaptable for large jazz and folk festivals as well as dance clubs, or any other environment. Some of his protégés, such as Buddy Guy, carry on these traditions today.

JOHN LEE HOOKER AND B.B. KING

Both John Lee Hooker and B.B. King had extremely long careers, both achieved initial success went through a fallow period before they were "discovered" by the white blues audience in the 1960s, in essence inaugurating new, second careers. Although now considered traditional blues artists, it is important to remember that they began as hitmakers on the R&B charts.

Hooker had a huge R&B hit called *Boogie Chillun* in 1949 on the Modern record label. Hooker's style was extremely simple and repetitious, and continued to be so during the next 51 years of his recording career. It was also quite dramatic, and easy to identify. For many of his early recordings a microphone was actually placed next to his foot, creating a sort of homemade drum sound. Many of Hooker's songs, including *Boogie Chillun*, had extended recitations. In the case of this particular tune, the song is a dialogue between a teenager and his mother about the young man's need to sow his wild oats. Hooker was "rediscovered" by the blues-rock group Canned Heat in the 1960s, and recorded an album with them, which introduced him to a young, white audience. He made several more "comebacks" over the next decades, often in association with blues revivalists such as Bonnie Raitt.

B.B. King is the exact musical opposite of Hooker. King has a very smooth guitar stylist, and uses some of his left-hand techniques on the electric guitar to simulate slide guitar playing, without its rough qualities. King bends the strings with his left-hand fingers, making the pitch of the string go up, and he also uses slides and tremolo effects. King's record career also began in 1949, but his first R&B hit was Lowell Fulson's song *Three O'Clock Blues*, recorded in 1951. Because both of these artists' careers spanned the period 1950–2000, and in King's case continues today, we will discuss them further in the next sections of this book.

THE RECORD BUSINESS IN POSTWAR AMERICA

Before we proceed to examine how rhythm and blues evolved outside of Chicago, we need to take a look at what was going on in the music business itself. By 1945, there were three major records labels, with a fourth newcomer soon to join the parade. The "big three" were Columbia, Decca, and RCA Victor, and the newcomer was Capitol, the first major label headquartered on the West Coast. By this time, all of these companies owned and operated their own recording studios, and the era of field recording for the majors had come to an end. Many of the people who worked for the majors came from a big band or swing background; this was the music they knew and loved. Many of the record producers had themselves been bandleaders, arrangers, or musicians. Consequently most of these men (and they were virtually all males) had little or no interest or background in the blues. A group of younger entrepreneurs, many of them more like riverboat gamblers than record executives, saw a window of opportunity to enter the business by specializing in black music. There were a half-dozen or so of these cowboy entrepreneurs who set the music business on its ear, initially by recording rhythm and blues, and soon after by entering the rock and roll arena.

Sam Phillips from Memphis was one of the most important of these people. He began recording such blues artists as Howlin' Wolf, James Cotton, Little Milton, and Doctor Ross. Phillips left the black music field when he decided to find "a white boy who could sing the blues," as he put it. He succeeded beyond his wildest dreams in accomplishing this end, recording Elvis Presley, and then Johnny Cash, Jerry Lee Lewis, and Carl Perkins, among others. In Cincinnati, Syd Nathan established King Records in 1945. Nathan's vision was a little different from Phillips's; from the beginning he recorded both rhythm and blues and country artists. Nathan owned the publishing rights to virtually everything he recorded, so he often had country and R&B artists make recordings of the same tunes. Among his early R&B artists were Wynonie Harris and Bull Moose Jackson, and the label even cut one hit song with blues-jazz guitarist Lonnie Johnson, a remake of a 1939 pop hit called *Tomorrow Night*. The label is probably best known for discovering and recording James Brown.

Another independent label was Imperial, run by Lew Chudd, whose major R&B artist was Fats Domino. Domino is a New Orleans piano player, singer, and songwriter who sold over forty million records during the 1950s and 1960s, and continues to perform today. In Los Angeles, the Bihari Brothers opened Modern Records, which recorded B.B. King, and Art Rupe founded Specialty Records, with R&B hitmakers including Lloyd Price, Guitar Slim, and, later, Little Richard. The Mesner Brothers checked in with Aladdin Records, recording bluesman Lightnin' Hopkins, and R&B acts Amos Milburn and Charles Brown.

We have already mentioned Chess Records in the discussion of Muddy Waters. This Chicago company was owned by Leonard and Phil Chess, Eastern European immigrants who entered the music business when they began managing a bar. In addition to their work with Muddy Waters, Howlin' Wolf, and Little Walter, Chess started recording Bo Diddley in 1955. Bo's trademark "shave and a haircut" rhythm had a foot in the blues and another in the R&B market-place. During the same year Chess released the first Chuck Berry recordings. Berry's guitar style was a sort of fusion of blues, jump blues, and boogie woogie elements, and he became known as one of the few black artists who was a rock and roll pioneer.

Another Chicago label, Mercury, was founded in 1945, and had enormous success with Dinah Washington. Washington had a gospel background, and she recorded a number of R&B and pop hits for the label from 1949 to 1960. Mercury became a very important record company, ranked in the tier just below the "big 4."

Several of the independent labels were owned by African Americans, notably Vee Jay in Chicago and Duke and Peacock in Houston. Vee Jay was owned by wife-and-husband team Vivian Carter Bracken and James Bracken, and Vivian's brother Calvin Carter. They first recorded bluesman Jimmy Reed in 1955. Reed's records featured his guitar and harmonica work, and he had a number of Top 10 R&B records from 1955 to 1961. Reed's records were really much closer to Chicago-style blues than to horn-and-rhythm-heavy R&B, but they made the R&B charts anyway.

Don Robey operated Duke and Peacock out of Houston. He recorded Louisiana bluesman-guitarist-fiddler Gatemouth Brown from 1948 to 1960, but most of Robey's artists were either gospel singers or more commercial R&B artists such as Johnny Ace and Bobby Blue Bland. Bland had 36 chart-making R&B songs between 1957 and 1970, but his singing owed more to gospel music than to the blues. The grittier Big Mama Thornton also recorded for the label, and she enjoyed one major hit, *Hound Dog,* in 1953; this song later became a hit for Elvis Presley.

Finally, Atlantic Records was founded by brothers Nesuhi and Ahmet Ertegun and partner Herb Abramson in 1947 in New York. The brothers were inveterate jazz fans, but quickly began to record rhythm and blues, achieving considerable success with Ruth Brown, and later doing even better with Ray Charles and Aretha Franklin. When Jerry Wexler joined the label in the mid-1950s, he became a key producer for its R&B artists, particularly working with Franklin in the 1960s.

Of all the record companies listed here, only Atlantic has remained under some of its original management, albeit as part of a much larger conglomerate. The other labels have long since been sold to other companies, and their records reissued on various labels. Atlantic successfully survived the transition to rock and roll, issuing records that crossed over to the white community by such artists as The Drifters, The Coasters, Ben E. King, and many others. In the 1960s, Atlantic moved into rock, signing Led Zeppelin, among others, and although it is now part of the Warner-Elektra-Atlantic group, Ahmet remains as one of the chief executives of the company.

Among the major labels, only Decca played a role in the development of R&B, primarily thanks to its savvy producer, Milt Gabler. Gabler recorded jump jazz bandleader Louis Jordan, starting in 1938. Jordan was the first black artist whose records crossed over to the pop charts. He generally recorded with a seven-piece combo, and he wrote much of his own material. Many of the songs were humorous novelty songs, such as *Five Guys Named Moe*, or *Is You Is or Is You Ain't My Baby*? Jordan's style was known as jump blues, a sort of swing-oriented, happy version of the blues, with most of the songs closer to popular music form than to traditional blues. Gabler also was one of the few major label producers who got in on rock and roll at an early date, producing Buddy Holly for Decca Records' subsidiary label Coral. Topping that off, Gabler was a catalyst for the recorded beginnings of the folk music revival, recording The Weavers for Decca.

With a few exceptions, the independent labels had rhythm and blues to themselves until the mid-1950s, when Columbia reactivated its Okeh label, RCA started a subsidiary called Groove, and Decca started a company called Brunswick. Although each of these labels experienced some success, notably Okeh with Jackie Wilson, considering that New York was certainly the central headquarters for the record business, it is surprising how many of the most successful R&B records were cut in Los Angeles, Chicago, New Orleans, Houston, and Cincinnati.

RHYTHM AND BLUES VS. THE BLUES

There are a number of differences between blues and rhythm and blues. Among the musical and lyric differences are the following:

- Blues songs generally had a twelve-bar structure. R&B music usually did not, instead using 8, 16, or even 32 bars. In this respect, R&B was closer to pop music.

- Because R&B records often utilized horns and larger groups, there was more evening-out of rhythms than is found in self-accompanied recordings by folk blues artists. The music on R&B recordings often featured partially or entirely written arrangements, something that rarely happened in folk blues recordings.
- Blues songs occasionally used refrains, but rarely used full choruses. R&B songs were much closer to pop songs, and utilized pop techniques, such as choruses, additional musical bridges, and lyrics that told a coherent story.
- Songwriters in R&B generally did not utilize lyrics that were found in other songs, while blues artists often dipped into traditional lyrics to fill out their songs. Occasionally, R&B songs were based on folk songs, such as *Staggerlee* or *Move To Kansas City*.
- Although the subject of romance was the most popular subject in traditional blues, it was virtually the only subject in R&B songs.
- R&B vocal styles had more variation than blues vocalists used. For example, many of the Los Angeles-based artists were crooners using pop vocal styles that derived from the work of Nat "King" Cole. Blues vocals generally were either impassioned or almost casual. (It should be mentioned that a few of the blues artists, such as Lonnie Johnson, moved back and forth between these vocal boundaries.)
- R&B showed a strong gospel influence in the use of growling, screaming, and falsetto vocal styles. There were indeed blues shouters, such as Jimmy Rushing or Joe Turner, but for the most part blues singers did not use these vocal styles. The use of better microphones and sound systems made it easier to execute these singing styles.
- Charley Patton and some other blues musicians were known for such gimmicks as playing the guitar behind their back, but R&B brought showmanship to a new level. Examples of this "showbiz" approach varied from tightly worked out choreography to such odd touches as saxophonist Screaming Jay Hawkins being carried onstage in a coffin.

TEXAS GOES TO CALIFORNIA: THE LA R&B SCENE

The black exodus from the south to California happened a little later than the Chicago population influx. From 1942 to 1945,

340,000 African Americans settled in California, 200,000 of them moving to Los Angeles. The attraction of California was that good-paying work was available in the aircraft and shipbuilding industries during World War II. A blues scene developed in Oakland that was rooted in Texas blues. Much of it was fueled by record producer-songwriter Bob Geddins, who recorded Lowell Fulson, K.C. Douglas, Jimmy McCracklin, and others. Geddins sometimes formed his own independent labels, and at other times he leased his recordings to Aladdin, Chess, and Modern Records. In Lee Hilderband's essay on Oakland blues in the book *California Soul: Music of African Americans in the West,* Geddins describes Oakland blues styles as having a "slow, draggier beat and a kinda mournful sound." Most of Geddins's artists played electric guitar, but their songs utilized folk blues forms as much as R&B song-writing techniques.

Meanwhile in Los Angeles, bandleader, songwriter, and drummer Johnny Otis was creating his own versions of rhythm and blues. Otis was a white man — of Greek descent — married to a black woman, who lived in the black community. He produced records with Little Esther, Johnny Ace, Etta James, and Big Mama Thornton, and wrote a number of R&B hits.

Los Angeles also pioneered another sort of R&B sound, one that was closer to white pop music. Various writers and musicians have described this style as more "laid back," and less aggressive than east coast or Chicago styles. This ballad style was popularized by pianist Cecil Gant with his 1945 giant hit *I Wonder*, and also utilized by Charles Brown in his 1946 hit *Drifting Blues*. The vocal styles and use of the piano and guitar owed a lot to the early recordings of the King Cole Trio, with its interplay of piano and jazz-oriented electric guitar blended with the smooth vocals of Nat "King" Cole. The vocals are relatively subdued and pleading, rather than aggressive or impassioned. The venues for the performance of these R&B ballads were more sophisticated lounges or supper clubs, as opposed to the more raucous environment where Chicago blues were played.

NEW YORK AND THE DOO-WOP GROUPS

The black migration to New York came primarily from the south-eastern states of Georgia, Florida, and the Carolinas. The music that evolved in New York was mostly doo-wop or unaccompanied vocal stylings. According to Arnold Shaw's authoritative *Honkers and Shouters: The Golden Years of Rhythm & Blues*, there were literally thousands of these groups on the streets of Harlem. Shaw lists a dozen groups that are little-known today, such as The Harptones, the Five Crowns, the Schoolboys, and The Jesters. There were a whole set of other groups named after cars, The El Dorados, The Fiestas, The Fleetwoods, Impalas, and the Imperials. Meanwhile, a plethora of small labels arose to record the fledgling doo-wop groups in the New York-New Jersey area, including Gee, Keynote, Variety, Beacon, Apollo, DeLuxe, Manor, Derby, and National, with Savoy in nearby New Jersey. Black entrepreneur-producer Bobby Robinson founded a number of labels, including Fire. These a cappella records had little relevance to the blues, and the singing was much more closely aligned with gospel music, especially in the melismatic vocal style, with a single word stretched out over several notes.

There were a few traditional bluesmen in the New York area, mostly performing for the nascent folk revival audience. Leadbelly came to New York in the late 1930s, and recorded for various small labels in the 1940s, notably for engineer-turned-record producer Moses Asch, who first founded Asch Records, then the Disc label, and finally, in 1947, Folkways Records. Folkways became a mainstay of the folk revival, and Asch recorded other local blues performers, notably Sonny Terry and Brownie McGee. The New Jersey-based jazz label Prestige started a blues subsidiary, Bluesville, in the late 1950s, and recorded many blues artists, including Rev. Gary Davis.

NEW ORLEANS

New Orleans became a major center for recording rhythm and blues, although the companies making the recordings there were virtually all from out of state. Authors John Broven and Jeff Hannusch have thoroughly documented the many successful R&B recordings from the scene. Virtually all of the recordings from 1945 until the 1960s centered around a small recording studio owned by Cosimo Matassa. Matassa also introduced the notion of a house rhythm section, a group of musicians who played on most of the sessions that were taking place. Later Sun and Stax Records in

Memphis, Motown in Detroit, and Philadelphia International in the Quaker City offered their own versions of this formula.

The biggest-selling New Orleans recordings were those of Fats Domino, arranged and orchestrated by trumpeter Dave Bartholomew. They had little to do with blues, but featured Fats' piano and his pleasant, laid-back vocals. Some other artists, such as Roy Brown, James Booker, and notably Guitar Slim, were more "down home," and they offered electric versions of the blues. Many of the New Orleans offerings had a kind of good-time feel to them, with a good deal of humor in the songwriting and performances. Examples are Ernie K. Doe's *Mother-in-Law* and Huey "Piano" Smith's *The Rockin' Pnuemonia and the Boogie Woogie Flu.*

To summarize and compare blues with its more commercial cousin, for rhythm and blues:

- Larger rhythm sections were utilized, especially adding a drummer.
- Many of the records used horns, especially a sort of honking tenor sax.
- The enunciation of the singers on the records tended to be clearer, and easier for white audiences to follow. The closer the singer was to performing blues the less this generalization held.
- The songs were commercial songs, with verses, choruses, and sometimes bridges, and they usually told a coherent story.

As time went on, the record companies became more and more eager for recordings to cross over to white audiences. This was not really a consideration in the blues of the 1920s and 1930s.

ROCK AND ROLL AND THE BLUES: 1954–1960

Beginning in the mid-1940s, the word "rock" made its appearance in a number of rhythm and blues songs. Charlie Gillett, in his excellent book *Sound of the City: The Rise of Rock and Roll*, mentions Roy Brown's recording of *Good Rockin' Tonight*, the song *Rock All Night Long*, recorded by many artists, and the 1951 Gunter Lee Carr dance record *We're Gonna Rock*. But rock and roll itself, as a musical style popular among white teenagers, awaited the appearance of Bill Haley's recording of *Crazy Man Crazy* in 1953. Haley was a country-swing musician who picked up on the idea of combining a modified rhythm and blues beat with a sort of white countryish musical feel.

It was Elvis Presley who brought rockabilly music to the attention of the American people. Rockabilly was a blues-oriented approach to country music, a genre that Sam Phillips at Sun Records in Memphis specialized in. Presley himself was a huge fan of rhythm and blues music, and in particular liked the work of Arthur "Big Boy" Crudup. Elvis's first record for Sun was Crudup's song *That's All Right*, backed with a 4/4-time, speeded-up version of Bill Monroe's bluegrass waltz *Blue Moon of Kentucky*. Presley's first five records for Sun all had an R&B song on one side of the two-sided records.

Through the 1950s, R&B artists' songs — and sounds — were shamelessly copied by white performers, who often achieved greater success with their "cover" versions than did the original artists. These cover records invariably cleaned up the words of the original to remove any taint of sexual innuendo. They generally speeded up the tempos, put less of an emphasis on the backbeat — the second and fourth beats of the measure — and the diction of the singers was easier for a white audience to understand. Cover versions were a stock-in-trade for early rock groups, beginning with Bill Haley's 1954 recording of *Shake, Rattle and Roll*, a laundered and slightly rewritten version of the original recording by Big Joe Turner. Elvis's versions were somewhat more original in nature. They were recorded with a slapped acoustic bass taking over the role of both the bass and the drums, and with guitarist Scotty Moore playing a combination of country and blues figures. Elvis was an explosive performer whose dance steps were regarded as sexually explicit. This led many older, more conservative figures — from religious pulpits to newspaper editorials — to denounce Elvis as a "bad influence" on America's youth.

Sun's other rockabilly artists, especially Johnny Cash, showed less direct rhythm and blues influence in their performances, although Jerry Lee Lewis's tunes owed a good deal to R&B performer Little Richard, and his songs were often structured like blues songs, with their repeated lines. Generally speaking most Sun recordings also showed a blues influence by featuring the guitar as the lead instrument. Carl Perkins in particular was a capable guitarist who was closer to the blues in his approach.

Although rockabilly shows blues influence of various extent, a good deal of rock and roll has less explicit connections with the blues. Chicago rhythm and blues, particularly the work of Chuck Berry and Bo Diddley, is probably the closest to blues of the various idioms of 1950s rock. The New York a cappella work, as we have already pointed out, has only a vague connection with the blues, and many of the later 1950s hits by such artists as Bobby Darin, Fabian, Frankie Avalon, and Bobby Rydell show little or no blues influence from either a songwriting or a performance perspective. The New Orleans dance blues of the 1950s have more of a Piedmont blues feel than the impassioned Delta style of performance. As we will soon see, it took the British rock and roll invasion of America in the 1960s to bring a whole new blues influence to rock and roll.

Summary

The period 1940–1960 showed profound changes in the blues. The Chicago blues initially added piano and bass to the mix, and by 1945 had introduced electric guitar and amplified harmonica. On the popular music front, rhythm and blues records, principally the recordings of Louis Jordan, started to cross over to the white audience. The end of World War II also saw the appearance of a number of independent record companies and individualistic entrepreneurs, who sought to capitalize on the growth of the African American population, and to spread the sound of the blues to the general American populace. By the mid-1950s, rock and roll began to penetrate the American airwaves, and to become the most important popular music style. There was some intersection between rock and blues, particularly in the Chicago blues artists and the Memphis rockabilly performers, but it took a new generation of rock performers in the 1960s to bring the blues firmly back into rock's style.

5

THE BLUES REVIVAL:
1960–1980

TIMELINE: 1960–1980

1960–1970	Numerous Civil Rights demonstrations, sit-is, voter registration drives and Freedom Rides occured
1961	Columbia Records released first Robert Johnson LP
1963	President John F. Kennedy assassinated
1964	Son House & Skip James performed at Newport Folk Festival
1968	Martin Luther King assassinated. Race riots followed in a number of cities, including Newark, Detroit and Philadelphia
1970	B.B. King's recording of *The Thrill is Gone* became a major R&B and pop hit *Living Blues* Magazine begans publishing
1973	Peace treaty with Vietnam signed
1979	First rap record appeared — *Rapper's Delight*, recorded by the Sugar Hill Gang
1974	President Richard Nixon resigns

In this chapter, we will show how the blues returned to prominence in American popular music, propelled by several separate, but related movements. The folk revival, which began in the late 1940s and blossomed in the later 1950s, helped bring renewed attention to acoustic blues performers. The revival inspired a new generation of scholars to search out many of the performers from the 1920s and 1930s, and to encourage them to begin playing the music again. And many folk revivalists themselves began specializing in acoustic blues. Beginning in the late 1950s, blues musicians began touring Europe, often sponsored by local jazz clubs. This inspired young musicians to take up the music, including a key group of players in London who met at a local club to swap songs and guitar licks. These musicians went on to form pop groups, including the Rolling Stones, the Yardbirds, and many others, who brought the music back to the United States. Several related movements in American music — notably the increased popularity of soul — also helped to reintroduce the blues aesthetic. And, in Chicago, the blues clubs continued to flourish, with older musicians such as Muddy Waters and Howlin' Wolf serving as mentors to a new generation of players.

THE FOLK REVIVAL

By the end of the 1950s, the rock and rock juggernaut that had dominated American popular music had slowed down drastically. Buddy Holly had died in an airplane crash, Jerry Lee Lewis's marriage to his 13-year-old cousin caused an uproar and derailed his career, and rock and roll had been infiltrated by such mainstream pop artists as Bobby Rydell, Fabian, and Frankie Avalon. This prepackaged teen-pop was designed to be commercially successful, but the songs themselves offered little for more sophisticated listeners — such as the college-aged audience — to enjoy. Such jazz artists as Dave Brubeck and Miles Davis appealed to this hipper crowd, but jazz music was too difficult for most amateur musicians to play. Folk music — with its intriguing message, yet easy-to-play melodies — offered an appealing alternative.

American folk music had experienced a brief run of popularity in the period 1949–1951, with a number of hit singles, including The Weavers's recording of Leadbelly's *Goodnight Irene*. However, because of their ties to left-wing politics, the Weavers' career ended when they ran foul of Cold War politics. Their records were removed from the airwaves, and their label, Decca, released the group from their contract. The folk revival appeared dead; however, in the late 1950s, a collegiate-looking group called The Kingston Trio recorded a song called *Tom Dooley*, an old Southern Appalachian ballad. To everyone's surprise the song became a giant hit single, and sparked a folk music revival, centered in America's colleges.

During this folk revival some other more roots-oriented artists such as Odetta, Bob Dylan, Joan Baez, and Judy Collins also began to appear in concert, and at outdoor venues such as the Newport Folk Festival. Pete Seeger, who had been the leader of The Weavers, began to experience new success as both a solo singer of folksongs and a songwriter. More than any other folk performer, Seeger encouraged his audiences to seek out the original artists whose songs he performed, and he also appeared in concerts with such blues performers as Big Bill Broonzy, and Brownie McGhee and Sonny Terry. Odetta and Dylan were both steeped in the blues traditions, and they began to spread the influence of the blues to their audiences, and to other aspiring performers.

THE STRANGE CAREER OF JOSH WHITE

Josh White had a peculiar, if underrated, role in the blues revival. Josh was originally from Greenville, South Carolina. His first recording sessions brought him to New York when he was a teenager, in 1931. By 1932, he had migrated to the city. White quickly developed a unique guitar style that virtually no one else has since imitated or taken up. It involved bending the strings with his left hand, while playing a number of original right-hand strums that involved almost South American-style string damping with his right palm. He also played up the neck of the guitar much more than many of the other bluesmen. White developed a loyal following in New York's small clubs, which appealed to an educated, liberal audience. White's charm, energy, and excellent diction, and his repertoire of songs about the chain gang, racial injustices, and even lynchings, made him very popular.

However, because of Josh's radical connections, he was mentioned in the late 1940s in a list of alleged communists and communist sympathizers called *Red Channels*. He appeared voluntarily before the House Committee on Un-American Activities, in 1950, and although he defended his antiracist leanings, he repudiated some of his radical connections, although he did not name anyone as being a communist, or claim that he had been recruited by anyone to join the party. After the hearings, Josh retained something of a career, but was in effect blacklisted by the left wing while still being spurned by more conservative listeners, and was not hired for some of the sorts of jobs for which he had previously been considered a natural choice.

Josh also was not particularly adopted in the blues revival by blues fans because his style was considered too slick and cosmopolitan. He did not dress, act, or perform like a rural black bluesman of the 1920s. Only Josh's son, Josh White Jr., has carried forward White's unique guitar style and general repertoire. He has toured widely since the early 1960s, but is a natural ballad and folksinger, so that blues do not form a major part of his repertoire.

BLUES SCHOLARSHIP AND REDISCOVERED BLUES SINGERS

There were three primary elements that fueled the blues revival of the 1960s:

- The rediscovery of a number of significant blues singers and songsters during the 1960s. These artists had recorded during the 1920s and 1930s, and had disappeared from the recording scene when the market for blues records dried up.
- The emergence of blues scholarship, beginning in 1959 with the publication of Samuel Charters' *The Country Blues*. Prior to Charter's book, the blues were always seen as one small part of American folksong, and appeared, for example, as sections of the folksong collections edited by John and Alan Lomax.
- The emergence of a number of young white blues enthusiasts who became professional musicians, and began to record and tour.

The "rediscovery" of original blues performers was carried out primarily by several record collectors and blues enthusiasts, mostly from the north, in the late 1950s and early 1960s. These collector-fans included Bill Barth, Ed Denson, John Fahey, Tom Hoskins, Dick Spottswood, Nick Perls, Henry Vestine, and Dick Waterman. In addition to locating the musicians, many of these blues aficionados went on to record or manage the artists, and Perls and Denson even started record companies. These "blues fanatics" combed the southern states in search of these original performers, and introduced them to the folk-revival audience. Often, they found clues in the original recordings made by the blues performers.

Mississippi John Hurt, for example, recorded an unusual song in his 1928 sessions for Okeh called *Avalon Blues*, stating in the chorus "Avalon, that's my home." Record collector Dick Spottswood was not sure if Hurt was simply picking up a well-known song or truly singing about his hometown. Following a hunch, he went to Avalon, Mississippi, where he discovered Hurt had been quietly living for years.

Although Hurt was primarily a songster who performed some blues, his rediscovery was followed in short order by various young white blues enthusiasts finding Skip James, Son House, Booker (Bukka) White, Reverend Robert Wilkins, and Buddy Moss. These were some of the great names in the history of Mississippi blues, and Moss was an excellent though somewhat neglected Piedmont blues artist. Other blues artists who reappeared on the scene included Furry Lewis in Memphis and Big Joe Williams in Chicago. The Rooftop Singers' hit record of *Walk Right In*, a jug band song written by Gus Cannon, brought him a briefly renewed recording career when Memphis soul recording label Stax produced one album with him.

The results of the blues revival for these "rediscovered" musicians varied. John Hurt enjoyed much more of a career after his discovery than he had during the time of his original recordings. He was in reasonably good health, and he sang and played as well as he ever had. Ironically, Hurt had never been a full-time professional musician. He used his reemergence as a springboard to improve his playing technique, and to become more comfortable at performing. Of all the rediscovered artists, he was probably the only one whose work actually improved on the original recordings. Bukka White, Skip James, and Son House all had a variety of health problems in their older years, and although they recaptured the feeling of their original artistry, their physical playing and singing skills had lost something over the years. Buddy Moss never seemed to capture the imagination of the young blues fans, and his rediscovery was just as frustrating to him as his original career had been.

Nonetheless, "new" blues performers continued to be "discovered" and promoted by collectors and blues fans. Artists began to turn up who had never had careers during the 1920s or 1930s, but who were excellent musicians with interesting repertoires. These included such musicians as Mance Lipscomb from Texas, John

Jackson from Virginia, Fred McDowell from Mississippi, and Robert Pete Williams from Louisiana.

Meanwhile, many of the same record collectors and enthusiasts began documenting the lives of the great blues performers, and also analyzed their music. Samuel Charters' 1959 book *The Country Blues* unleashed a whole flood of books about the blues. English blues scholar Paul Oliver wrote a series of books about the blues beginning with his 1960 *Blues Fell This Morning*. Oliver's work included biographical sketches, interviews with blues artists, and transcriptions of blues lyrics. Oliver went on to edit a whole series of small books about numerous blues artists and blues subjects, such as the blues revival, and African musical retentions in the blues. The only black author to write about the blues during this time was Leroi Jones, whose *Blues People: Negro Music in White America* was published in 1963. Jonathan Sackheim's *The Blues Line* appeared in 1969, reprinting over 500 blues lyrics. Oliver and Louisiana folklorist Harry Oster also made collecting trips in the South, finding still more blues artists in the course of their travels. Folklorist Charles Keil was the first scholar to focus on the electric blues, in his 1966 book *Urban Blues*.

PROTEST MUSIC AND THE BLUES

Various scholars have different attitudes about whether or not the blues qualify as protest music. Charters had a kind of idealistic and romanticized attitude toward the blues, and he insisted that the blues were about romantic love, and only rarely touched on social protest. At the same time, he reprinted lyrics that clearly contradicted his point of view. Other scholars saw the blues as protest of an indirect nature, commenting on the singer's lot in a variety of contexts, ranging from love and sex to imprisonment or poverty. Still others saw the blues as a kind of surrealist view of life, where a subversive view of the power structure was encouraged, without a direct call to social action. A Dutch scholar named Guido Van Rijn analyzed blues lyrics of the 1930s and 1940s in his book *Roosevelt's Blues: African-American Blues and Gospel Songs on FDR*. Van Rijn found 349 songs that included some form of political commentary in the approximately 25,000 gospel and blues songs recorded from 1902 to 1945, or about 1.6 percent of the total. Most of the political commentary was found in the blues, with only a handful of gospel songs including political sentiments.

Into this odd mix can be thrown the work of Lawrence Gellert, a New York writer who moved to North Carolina for medical reasons. Between 1924 and 1937, he recorded 500 black protest songs in the southern United States, publishing two folios of songs. Eventually three albums were issued from his collection, and the original recordings are in an archive at Indiana University. Of his published and recorded songs, many are work songs, but quite a few are blues. Gellert seems to have gained the confidence of his informants by guaranteeing them anonymity, and because he was living with a black woman. No other scholar or folklorist has collected anywhere near this number of protest songs. Until someone does a complete and thorough analysis of Gellert's collection, it is probably best to say that although the majority of blues songs are about love, romance, and sex, there indeed have been a number of them that criticize the white man, and protest the social conditions of African Americans. Blues focus on autonomy and independence, and given the social conditions for African Americans during the time the music began and flourished, one can make a good argument that the very existence of the music was a protest against the dominant culture.

Originally scholars were skeptical of Gellert's findings, and some thought that he had written all of these songs himself. One of the problems that scholars had in dealing with the work was that in order to gain his informants' confidence, Gellert kept no field notes on the names of the artists that he recorded, or exactly where he had found the songs. It is interesting to contrast his methods with the way that John and Alan Lomax went about their work. There are field recordings of John Lomax practically attempting to coerce Blind Willie McTell into singing protest songs, and getting a puzzled response from McTell. Lomax was a white Texan, and conservative politically, so that it is not too surprising that his informants did not totally trust him. Even his son Alan, who was more politically radical and sympathetic to the artists, was still generally being sent to collect songs by a government agency, and one would imagine that his informants did not entirely trust him either. Alan Lomax did record an album called *Blues in the Mississippi Night*, where he conducts a sort of verbal jam session with a group of (initially) un-named black artists where they talk about their experiences with racism and the Jim Crow system. This album was made with a group of professional musicians who had some relationship with Lomax, as opposed to a group of chain gang prisoners who were setting eyes on him for the first time.

We should also factor into this discussion the protest songs that such artists as Big Bill Broonzy, Leadbelly, and Josh White performed and recorded. All of these artists had fairly extensive contact with radical white Americans, and many scholars have taken the position that these songs were written because their audiences actually wanted to hear them. In other words, in a sense they were the equivalent of songs written for commercial purposes. Big Bill Broonzy wrote a song called *Black, Brown and White* Blues, pointing out the values of white, or at least light-brown skin coloring. Josh White even recorded several of Gellert's songs, and with poet Waring Cuney wrote quite a few of his own, recording an entire album called *Chain Gang*. He continued to perform songs highlighting social inequality throughout his long career.

Leadbelly spent the last 15 years of his life in New York, and was quite popular with left-wing political groups. We mentioned his song *Bourgeois Blues* earlier in the book (see Chapter 3). This was a song about Leadbelly and his wife trying to find a place to stay in Washington, D.C., that would accept both of them, and would also accommodate Alan Lomax and his wife. As the song tells the story, the places that would accept the white couple would not allow the black couple to stay there, and vice versa. Leadbelly sardonically commented that Washington was a "bourgeois town," a term that he might have learned from Lomax or from his own experiences performing at left-wing rallies with such political artists as Pete Seeger and Woody Guthrie. Leadbelly also wrote songs praising the war effort and denouncing Hitler, in much the same way that Seeger and Guthrie did.

In the 1960s, Chicago bluesman J.B. Lenoir wrote a number of topical political songs, on such subjects as Eisenhower, the Korean War, the Civil Rights movement, and the war in Vietnam. Lenoir was more popular in Europe than in his hometown of Chicago. One can only speculate on his motivations for writing these songs, but there appears to be no reason to doubt his sincerity.

THE YOUNG, WHITE BLUES SINGERS

The folk revival inspired renewed interest in blues performers, particularly in New York City. Artists who had already established a presence on the New York scene, particularly Gary Davis and Brownie McGhee and Sonny Terry, suddenly drew young, white blues enthusiasts like a magnet. Davis and McGhee both acquired a number of white students, and McGhee and Terry began to tour colleges and folk festivals not only in the United States, but overseas as well. Young guitarist Happy Traum studied with McGhee, and transcribed a number of his solos, which were published in a popular instruction book. Another young guitarist named Stefan Grossman spent years studying with Davis, transcribed his music, recorded him in informal situations, and published several instruction books that detailed Gary's unique guitar style. Grossman went on to transcribe the solos of numerous other blues artists, ranging in style from ragtime pickers to slide guitarists. Guitarist Jerry Silverman wrote his master's thesis on Josh White, and transcribed quite a lot of his recorded work, wrote an early blues guitar instruction manual, and taught dozens of aspiring guitarists.

The last piece of the puzzle emerged in the performances and recordings of a number of young, white blues guitarists and singers. On the New York scene, gravel-voiced singer-guitarist Dave Van Ronk became a popular figure, beginning with two albums for Folkways in the late 1950s, and then several more for the slightly larger Prestige label. Also in New York, John Hammond Jr., the son of the famous record producer, began playing blues, and Stefan Grossman was a regular on the scene. Jug band music was revived by the short-lived Even Dozen Jug Band, which featured Grossman, Steve Katz, John Sebastian, and Maria Muldaur, among others. Katz would partner with another guitarist, Danny Kalb, to found the group The Blues Project (despite its name, it was more of a rock-improvisational group than a blues band). Later on, members of this group went on to form Blood, Sweat, and Tears, a successful rock band of the early 1970s that showed the influences of blues and big band jazz. Sebastian founded the Lovin' Spoonful, a band that showed strong folk influences; and the Spoonful even recorded a song in homage to eccentric Texas songster Henry Thomas (who had cut 78s with his own guitar and panpipe accompaniment in the 1920s).

Another center of the folk revival was Boston, where a number of musicians took up the blues. Artist-musician Eric Von Schmidt was a fixture on the scene. Tom Rush, before he became a singer-songwriter, recorded blues material. Jim Kweskin formed a jug band in Boston that featured a number of people who were important individual musicians in their own right. They included blues musicians Geoff and Maria Maudaur, and (later) pioneering banjo picker Bill Keith. Both Geoff and Maria continue to perform today. Both of them have unusual voices, and Geoff is also a talented arranger.

The folk revival spread to many other cities, and with it went an interest in the blues. Minneapolis blues enthusiasts John Koerner, Dave Ray, and Tony Glover formed a blues trio in the early 1960s, recording several albums for Elektra beginning in 1963. Glover wrote an influential guide to playing blues harmonica, which remains in print today. California also spawned several blues revivalists, including Ry Cooder, a Los Angeles teenager who soon emerged as a world-class bottleneck guitarist and composer, and San Francisco Bay region singer Barbara Dane, one of the first white women to sing the blues. Mark Spoelstra, another California blues aficionado, played excellent six- and twelve-string guitar in his own version of the Piedmont style. Oddly, very few of the blues revivalists were black, but among these few Bruce Langhorne and Larry Johnson were on the New York scene, Jerry Ricks started to build a reputation in Philadelphia, and Taj Mahal began a lengthy career that ranged from blues to world music styles.

Chicago, with its vibrant electric blues scene, inspired a different type of blues revivalist. Local harmonica player Paul Butterfield formed one of the first interracial blues bands, using Howlin' Wolf's rhythm section. Guitarists who played with Butterfield over the years included Michael Bloomfield and Elvin Bishop, both of whom became major figures in the blues-rock scene of the late 1960s to early 1970s. Bloomfield and Butterfield learned much of their repertoire by going to South Side Chicago blues clubs, and eventually by sitting in with such masters of the blues as Muddy Waters. Because Butterfield, Bloomfield, and company were modeling themselves after artists who had bands and played in loud clubs, they had more of a rhythm and blues influence than the East Coast revivalists, who were more oriented towards the country blues artists. The Chicago group was in effect modeling its music after the black masters of the idiom in the same way that young white Chicago jazz musicians, including Benny Goodman and Bud Freeman, went to the black nightclubs to hear and emulate the work of jazz stars Louis Armstrong and King Oliver in the late 1920s.

All of the white revivalists were steeped in the blues, and performed songs by the major country blues artists. In some instances, they performed note-for-note renditions of the original recordings; in other cases they attempted to capture the general style of the original artist without precisely imitating them. In general, the white players served up fairly creditable renditions of the originals, except for their vocals. It was more difficult to imitate the vocal strength and the subtle inflections of the original blues artists. The younger artists seemed to gravitate more toward reproducing instrumental styles than toward capturing the passion and power inherent in blues vocals. Part of it was sheer vocal talent; part of it was capturing subtleties of inflection and other vocal stylistic mannerisms. Most of the early white revivalists primarily performed traditional songs, although some, such as Koerner, Ray and Glover, performed original songs in a blues style.

Oddly the white blues guitarists have received virtually no coverage by blues scholars. The three books currently in print on the folk music and blues revivals barely mention them, and although there are an increasing number of books that detail the history of the blues, only Michael Bane's *White Boy Singing' the Blues: The Black Roots of White Rock* deals with the white artists in some detail. Bane includes a chapter on Michael Bloomfield, Paul Butterfield, and the Chicago blues. At the time of writing, Elijah Wald is editing a collection of the writings of New York white blues artist Dave Van Ronk, which should remedy some of this neglect. Coverage of the British blues artists, as we will shortly see, is a different matter.

Soon a number of younger female white artists also started to perform and record. The most famous of these blues women was Janis Joplin, who joined the band Big Brother and the Holding Company in San Francisco. Joplin ultimately became a major rock star, using her blues shouting as her platform. Tracy Nelson was another blues-influenced singer who briefly fronted a rock band, Mother Earth, in the late 1960s and early 1970s. She has returned to performing with a more traditional blues accompaniment over the past decades. Two San Francisco Bay singer-musicians, Terry Garthwaite and Toni Brown, formed a blues-rock band called The Joy of Cooking and recorded several successful albums for Capitol. On the more acoustic side of things Judy Roderick and Alice Stuart recorded acoustic blues for Vanguard and Arhoolie Records. Roderick was a talented singer whose career swung between recording jazz (for Columbia Records) and blues, and folk rock for Atlantic Records.

Perhaps the most influential of the female blues-rockers was singer-songwriter Bonnie Raitt, who came out of the Boston blues revival scene. Her first album was recorded at John Koerner's home studio, and focused strongly on a blues-based repertoire. An excellent slide guitarist, Raitt has gone on to record a wide range of material, but has always acknowledged the blues as a key influence on her music. Rory Bloch, a New York singer and guitarist studied blues guitar assiduously, and began recording when she was only a teenager. She continues her career today, mixing Delta blues with her own songs.

THE NEW INDEPENDENT RECORD LABELS

Although the market for the Chicago electric blues continued to be the black buyer of 45 rpm singles, a group of record labels reissued long-playing records of the famous country blues recordings, and even recorded some new material, and in some case new artists. In the 1950s, Riverside Records reissued the recordings of Blind Lemon Jefferson, Ma Rainey, and others. Moe Asch's Folkways Records, in addition to reissuing albums by such artists as Leadbelly, recorded new albums by Brownie McGhee and Big Bill Broonzy, and recorded young white blues singer Dave Van Ronk. In the later 1950s, Asch founded a related label, RBF, to feature reissues of blues and jazz recordings; Sam Charters edited an album of blues 78s to accompany his 1959 book *The Country Blues* as the first RBF release. Various blues collectors founded new labels, such as Chris Strachwitz's Arhoolie Records, originally founded to release field workings that Strachwitz made of Texas songster Mance Lipscomb, Bob Koester's Delmark Records in Chicago, and such other labels as Prestige/Blueville, Herwin Records, the Origin

Jazz Library, Testament Records, Yazoo Records, and classic blues singer Victoria Spivey's Spivey Records. Folk label Vanguard also jumped in, with a series of Chicago blues releases, and later with recordings of white blues artists Judy Roderick and Lisa Kindred. Some of the companies operated on a shoestring, and the actual sound of the reissued recordings was scratchy and difficult to listen to. Often the reissued recordings were extremely rare, and the master tapes were copied from old 78 rpm releases.

Another source for blues fans was late-night radio, where 50,000 watts, clear channel stations could be heard many miles beyond their daytime range. After sundown many of the daytime stations went off the air, allowing these powerful stations to be heard in distant cities. WLAC in Nashville, in particular, with DJ John Richbourg, introduced country blues and R&B recordings to many young white listeners, and commercials for mail-order record stores offered to sell the recordings to the listeners. WVON in Chicago was another station that leaned heavily on the blues in its programming, as did WDIA in Memphis.

WHY THE BLUES BECAME POPULAR?

During the 1960s, many young white people were fascinated by the sound of the blues, and also by what the blues represented. To white, middle-class listeners, the blues had an element of rebellion that was both social and sexual. The blues talked about sex, not romance, and it also highlighted the dynamics of a culture that was relatively exotic to the middle-class, white listener. The dilemmas discussed in blues songs — failed romances, hard times, and traveling to new and unknown destinations — were all fascinating to the mostly college-age audiences.

The guitar had become increasingly popular by this time, thanks to both the folk revival and its role in rock and roll. Blues guitar offered another approach, and it was attractive to many listeners who became amateur guitarists. More demanding than the simple strumming of folk or rock licks, the blues style offered new challenges for guitarists who wanted to go beyond simple chord work. It also allowed them to "show off" their instrumental virtuosity.

In addition to the medium of records, there were folk clubs spread out across the United States that often featured blues artists. These included The Ash Grove in Los Angeles, the Second Fret in

Philadelphia, Mother Blues in Chicago, Club 47 in Cambridge, Massachusetts, and the Village Gate and Gerde's Folk City in New York. Young listeners who would never have dreamed of going to the tough South Side clubs of Chicago could come to these clubs and hear their favorite blues artists, or be introduced to new ones. There were also blues festivals, starting with a 3-day festival in Ann Arbor, Michigan, in 1969. Chicago picked up the challenge with its own festival. The blues also could be seen and heard as an important ingredient of such festivals as the annual Newport Folk Festivals of the 1960s. By the mid- to late 1960s, live blues music was readily available to the listener of any color, in a safe listening environment, whether on records or live.

THE BLUES GOES ABROAD

In the mid-1950s, the Chris Barber Band sparked enthusiasm for Dixieland jazz and blues in Britain. Banjoist Lonnie Donegan left the Barber Band and recorded his version of Leadbelly's *Rock Island Line*. The song became a huge hit in both Great Britain and the United States, and spawned a British version of American folk music called "skiffle." Skiffle was sort of a British version of jug band music. Many young British musicians took to forming skiffle groups, among them a teenaged John Lennon. Donegan's recording of *Rock Island Line* was not exactly a blues, and Leadbelly himself was more of a songster than a blues artist, but it was a beginning.

Before Donegan left the Barber Band, he was called up to military service, and the person who replaced him in the group was Alexis Korner. In 1962, Korner briefly opened up a blues club in London, in partnership with drummer Cyril Scott. The club quickly closed, but the two then started a band called Blues Incorporated. The club and then the band became centers for a number of would-be blues musicians, including singers Long John Baldry and John Mayall, both future blues band leaders, and a few scruffy younger blues fans, including singer Mick Jagger and guitarist Keith Richard — who would soon form their own blues-rock band, The Rolling Stones, named after a Muddy Waters song. Soon afterwards bassist Jack Bruce and drummer Ginger Baker, later to become members of the rock group Cream, and future Rolling Stone Ron Wood were involved in various blues bands.

John Mayall started a band called The Bluesbreakers in 1963, and he was able to recruit a young British guitarist named Eric Clapton in 1965. Clapton in turn was replaced in The Bluesbreakers by Jeff Beck and Jimmy Page, both of whom were excellent blues players, but were not as deeply committed to the blues idiom as Clapton was. Other people who passed through Mayall's bands include John McVie, Mick Fleetwood, and Bob Brunning — who later were founding members of Fleetwood Mac — guitarist Peter Green, also to join Fleetwood Mac, Mick Taylor — who briefly replaced Brian Jones in The Rolling Stones in the late 1960s to early 1970s — and inventive acoustic guitarist Davey Graham, one of the trailblazers in playing and composing fingerstyle acoustic guitar music.

The British blues artists were much more influenced by the Mississippi Delta blues than most of their young American counter- parts were. Specifically, it was the Chicago adaptations of the Delta blues that appealed to them, with the electric guitar, amplified harmonica, and intense slide guitar leads. Unlike the young American white artists of the early 1960s, many of these British musicians became major rock stars. As such they wielded tremendous influence over their audiences. They freely acknowledged the influ- ences of their heroes, such as Muddy Waters, Howlin' Wolf, and Robert Johnson, and they recorded some of their songs, and in a number of cases used blues artists as their opening acts. However, some blues-rockers took authorship credit for songs they learned from the older bluesmen, or attributed the songs to "traditional" or "public domain" authorship. This practice was common in the music industry, but denied important author royalties to many of the older artists — many of whom desperately needed the income.

But not all of the blues rockers failed to give credit to their mentors. Eric Clapton, in particular, over the years has recorded many blues songs, and has made it a point to credit the originators of the music. Clapton's recording of Skip James' *"I'm So Glad"*, recorded when Clapton was a member of the power trio Cream, was a huge shot in the arm for James; royalties from the recording paid James's medical expenses at a time when he was virtually destitute. The homage that the British acts paid to the bluesmen was not only monetary. The Yardbirds and The Animals both recorded with Sonny Boy Williamson (#2; aka Rice Miller), and several of the British acts went to Chicago and recorded at the Chess studios, including The Rolling Stones. Apparently, they felt that some of Muddy Waters's and Howling Wolf's magic would rub off on them.

The biggest difference between the British and American white revivalists was in their vocal sounds. Many of the young Americans simply did not have the vocal equipment to compete with such artists as Muddy Waters. Eric Burden of The Animals and a young British singer-keyboard player named Stevie Winwood had a great deal of vocal firepower, and they were not particularly imitative of the traditional American bluesmen. They were able to come up with their own style that wed the intensity and emotion of blues singing to their own experiences.

Another important difference is that many of the Americans, including Koerner, Ray, and Glover and John Hammond Jr., were modeling themselves after the country blues artists, while many of the British artists were more enamored of rhythm and blues styles, rather than folk blues. Stevie Winwood's performances with the Spencer Davis group of such tunes as *Keep on Running*, were really closer to Ray Charles's work than to Muddy Waters's style. The same could be said of Eric Burden's performance of *The House of the Rising Sun*, which seemed to be based on Dave Van Ronk's guitar arrangement, but which erupted into Burden's impassioned "hollering" toward the end of the song.

Most of these British blues-rock artists first appeared during the 1960s, but Led Zeppelin sparked another British blues invasion, beginning in 1970. Zeppelin recorded a number of early blues tunes, such as Robert Johnson's *Travelling Riverside Blues* and Memphis Minnie's *When the Levee Breaks*. Unlike Clapton, Zeppelin managed to cut themselves in as cowriters and publishers of these songs, which they clearly arranged but did not write. In the case of several other songs, they claimed that the songs were traditional and copyrighted them in their own names. Despite this less-than-laudable behavior, the band did introduce real blues songs to their large audience.

The British blues revival was fueled by several tours made by American artists, beginning with two appearances by Muddy Waters in the later 1950s. Big Bill Broonzy also made several European tours, including British performances, in this period. By the 1960s, there was a veritable flood of touring American artists, including John Lee Hooker, Howlin' Wolf, Little Walter, Buddy Guy,

Brownie McGhee and Sonny Terry, and Arthur "Big Boy" Crudup. In a number of cases, British musicians served as the rhythm section for these players, creating a very direct musical influence on the younger musicians' music. Many of the older blues artists were shocked at the respect that they received in Britain and in Europe. They were asked to autograph recordings that they barely remembered making, and in general were treated as artists, rather than hired hands. A number of the visiting musicians subsequently moved to Europe, including Memphis Slim, who relocated to Paris, Curtis Jones, who moved to Copenhagen, and Champion Jack Dupree, who moved to England.

There were quite a few other British artists who were part of the British blues scene. Christine Perfect, later McVie, sang in both Chicken Shack and Fleetwood Mac, and Maggie Bell was the dynamic singer in the band Stone the Crows. Jo-Anne Kelly, who focused on country blues in her repertory, made a number of recordings, some with various bands, some with her brother Dave Kelly, and even made a recording in the United States followed by an American tour. Rory Gallagher had a successful rock-blues band, and Gallagher and Alex McEwen were fine acoustic guitarists, Rory and Alex McEwen never achieved any great fame.

AMERICAN BLUES-ROCK BANDS

The mid-1960s saw the arrival of the American blues bands, notably Canned Heat. The band was founded by blues aficionados and record collectors. Al Wilson had played guitar on some mid-1960s Son House recordings, and was also a superb harmonica player. Bob Hite was an intense lead singer with a gruff sound, while Wilson had a softer, almost spoken vocal approach. They played a number of traditional tunes, as well as recording tunes by Muddy Waters and other blues and R&B artists. The band had several big hit records, and in 1969 recorded an album with blues legend John Lee Hooker, titled *Hooker 'n' Heat*. However, Wilson died in 1970, and the band was not able to sustain its popularity.

Many of the American rock bands, psychedelic and otherwise, showed blues influences or at least traces of blues in their recordings. Some of the younger blues players, such as Ry Cooder and Bruce Langhorne, played on numerous recordings, and even on film scores.

Studio musicians such as Eric Gale and Cornell Dupree also brought blues guitar influences to many pop and soul records of the 1970s.

JIMI HENDRIX

Jimi Hendrix was an American R&B guitarist who had toured in the early 1960s as a member of the backup bands for Little Richard and the Isley Brothers. In the mid-1960s, he was performing in Greenwich Village for virtually no money, when he was brought to England by The Animals' bass player Chas Chandler. Chandler hired two British musicians to perform with Hendrix, naming the group the Jimi Hendrix Experience, and Hendrix became a superstar. Hendrix was a spectacular electric guitar player, who was fascinated by technology. He was constantly introducing electronic sounds, such as feedback and the use of various foot pedals. He actually used volume as a form of intentional distortion.

Hendrix developed confidence in his singing and writing through the music of Bob Dylan, and he returned to the United States as a rock star. What Hendrix introduced to blues (and rock) was the notion of using distortion as an expressive musical tool. His performances also were quite spectacular. He used the devices of playing with his teeth, playing behind his back, and literally destroying the guitar at the end of his performances. Although Hendrix had transformed himself from a blues musician into a rock superstar, some of his musical innovations influenced the electric blues. This influence has lasted long after his career was cut short by his premature death.

BLACK GOSPEL MUSIC

Gospel music is composed religious music. As spirituals moved onto the concert stage, a new impetus to create religious music was born. The man considered to be the father of the movement was Thomas A. Dorsey, who had enjoyed a career in blues as Ma Rainey's pianist-band leader, and as Tampa Red's partner (performing under the name of "Georgia Tom"; see Chapters 2 and 3). Dorsey and Tampa performed quite a lot of music filled with double entendres during the 1920s. Dorsey became transformed into a religious composer when his wife was struck with a serious illness in the

1930s. A community of powerful singers developed around him, including Mahalia Jackson and Roberta Martin. Dorsey sold his music in churches, and several of his songs, such as *Take My Hand, Precious Lord,* became enormously successful. Dorsey's astonishingly long career lasted until his death in 1993.

There are several books that are entirely devoted to gospel music, notably Tony Heilbut's *The Gospel Sound: Good News and Bad Times,* but our concern here is simply to discuss some of the influences of gospel music that filtered into soul and American popular music in partnership with the blues. The vocal style of gospel music is extremely impassioned, and utilizes the highest and lowest ranges of its singers' capabilities. The high falsetto parts, mastered by such singers as Curtis Mayfield, were made possible by the development of sophisticated microphones. Another characteristic of gospel music was the use of extensive harmony singing, a trait virtually unknown in the blues. Male vocal quartets and quintets such as The Dixie Hummingbirds or The Five Blind Boys of Alabama were particularly noted for their vocal harmonies. As with the classic blues of the 1920s, many of the most powerful and musically significant solo gospel singers have been women. Mahalia Jackson, Roberta Martin, Clara Ward, Sallie Martin, Marian Williams, and Shirley Caesar are among the many who belong on such a list.

Many of the famous R&B and soul singers, including Sam Cooke, Ray Charles, Aretha Franklin, and Otis Redding, had vocal styles that married the music of the blues with gospel-influenced embellishments. Ray Charles was probably the first singer to achieve broad popularity who displayed vocal roots in gospel, but when soul music developed, virtually every major singer displayed an obvious background in gospel music.

SOUL MUSIC

There is not really a specific difference between rhythm and blues and soul music. There are some guideposts that we can set up that should help to explain the evolution of black popular music and how its relationship to the blues changed. R&B utilized instrumental resources that were derived from the blues, specifically the way that the Delta blues was transformed in Chicago. The music was often played by small combos, with guitar or saxophone usually playing the leads. However, the vocal style of soul music was closer to gospel music than to the blues, including the use of falsetto singing, bass vocals, and vocal harmony.

Peter Guralnick's excellent book *Sweet Soul Music: Rhythm and Blues and the Southern Dream of Freedom* describes soul music as emerging in 1960, crossing over into pop music in the mid-1960s, and running its course by the early 1970s. He makes the point that soul was really a southern music style, while R&B evolved in a number of places, especially in Los Angeles, Chicago, and New York. Two southern towns played a key role in the development of soul music, Memphis, Tennessee, and Muscle Shoals, Alabama, thanks to two influential recording studios, Stax Records in Memphis and Muscle Shoals Sound in Alabama. Oddly, in both of these places, many of the musicians recording the backup tracks were white, although almost all of the singers were black. Booker T and the MGs were a popular band who made some hit records on their own, and they were also the rhythm section who played on most of the hits coming out of Stax Records in Memphis. The band was integrated that drummer Al Jackson and keyboard virtuoso Booker T. Jones were black, and guitar player Steve Cropper and bass player Duck Dunn were white. The producers and the songwriters were also a mix. The Muscle Shoals rhythm section was entirely white, but the musicians had all grown up on R&B music, and they preferred it to country music.

The Stax vocalists included Sam and Dave, Otis Redding, and Carla and Rufus Thomas. Atlantic Records, fresh from its triumphs with Ray Charles, came down to Memphis, and later to Muscle Shoals, and brought Aretha Franklin, Solomon Burke, Wilson Pickett, and others to record in these studios. All of these artists had a background in gospel music, and their performance style was akin to the performance of southern preachers. The background singers often sang short phrases that contained excerpts of a song's lyrics, in a sort of call-and-response pattern with the lead singer. A perfect example of this is Aretha Franklin's sisters' vocal responses in her recording of Otis Redding's song *Respect*; sometimes they simply sing the syllables "re-re-re," and in other parts of the song they sing "just a little bit, just a little bit."

Many of the songs that these artists recorded were written by the various musicians and producers who worked on the sessions.

When New York record producer Jerry Wexler brought his Atlantic artists down south, the musical arrangements that evolved on these southern sessions were "head arrangements," spontaneous musical arrangements that were not written out note-for-note, but were improvised by musicians on the recording sessions. This was possibly the musical element on these recordings that was closest to the blues, and the way that they were recorded in Chicago during the late 1940s and early 1950s. In New York, most session musicians read charts that a musical arranger had constructed.

In Chicago, producer Carl Davis and producer-songwriter-guitarist-vocalist Curtis Mayfield introduced the element of social concern into soul music, with such songs as 1965's *People Get Ready*. Mayfield had a light falsetto voice, and again his music was much closer to gospel music than to blues, with the occasional blues guitar riff adding some color to the proceedings. The same might be said of James Brown, whose recordings became increasingly popular in the 1960s, with his gruff preacher-like delivery and his dynamic stage show. Late in the 1960s, producers Kenneth Gamble and Leon Huff took the soul sound, and added big-band string and horn arrangements, coming up with the so-called Philly Soul style. Although social concerns were sometimes addressed in their productions, the music was far afield from the blues. By the mid-1970s disco had entered the scene, and the use of synthesizers and drum machines took the music even further away from any trace of the blues.

BUILDING A NEW BLUES AUDIENCE

Beginning with the rock and roll revolution of the mid-1950s, it became increasingly difficult for blues artists to compete in the popular music marketplace. Meanwhile, the R&B charts were dominated by soul and its musical offspring, as well as the powerful pop sounds coming out of Detroit's Motown label. By the later 1950s, artists such as Muddy Waters and Howlin' Wolf could no longer make the R&B charts, and the younger blues-oriented artists, especially Chuck Berry, were writing and performing songs that were closer to rock-pop songs than to blues. In Berry's case, the subject matter of the songs was also designed to appeal to teenagers, focusing on such subjects as cars and dances. According to Leadbitter and Slaven's discography, the number of blues singles declined from a high of 320 in 1949 to 90 in 1966. Motown began to explode on the scene in the early 1960s, but most of the Motown recordings were designed for white teenagers, and offered only small dollops of soul, usually in the vocal performances of such artists as Martha and The Vandellas or The Four Tops.

Of course, there were always a few exceptions to the saccharine musical offerings of Motown on other record labels, such as Jimmy Reed's success, or the soul-oriented recordings of blues guitarist Albert King and the instrumentals of Freddie King. But artists such as Muddy Waters and Howlin' Wolf were regarded as being old-fashioned by the younger black record buyer. The pendulum began to swing in the mid- to late 1960s, when white rock fans were introduced to such performers as Muddy Waters and B.B. King, and became a new audience for their music. In 1970, B.B. King scored his first giant crossover hit, *The Thrill Is Gone*, and for the first time in his career he began to develop a large and appreciative white audience.

LOUISIANA BLUES: THE SOUND OF THE SWAMP

A group of Louisiana blues artists emerged during the 1960s. They recorded on the Excello label, owned and operated by recording engineer Jay Miller, who worked out of a small studio in Crowley, Louisiana. Miller was also a songwriter, and wrote a number of the songs that these artists recorded. He also cowrote with some of the artists. Slim Harpo, Lightnin' Slim, Lazy Lester, and Lonesome Sundown were a few of the artists whom Miller recorded. These records all use relatively sparse instrumentation, with electric guitar and harmonica usually featured as the solo instruments. Occasionally, saxophone or piano parts are also thrown into the mix. The records also feature prominent drum parts, hitting hard on the second and fourth beats of the measure. Most of these artists were used to playing in tough southern jook joints, where it was necessary to play electric guitar to be heard amidst the general clamor of drinking, dancing, and partying. The electric guitar styles blended elements of B.B. King's string-bending and occasional touches of John Lee Hooker's echo-filled style. The harmonica is used to play straight melody, not for rhythmic purposes.

Miller's musical input led to some of the artists recording everything from country and western tinged ballads to rockabilly tunes, as well as the more typical rhythm and blues numbers. Some of these artists were white, and obviously encouraged by Miller to rekindle the rockabilly sounds of Sun Records, although they were recorded 5 to 10 years after the heyday of the Memphis rockabilly sound.

Oddly, just as the blues was moving into a more sophisticated musical genre, the very rawness of these records seemed to generate a certain amount of popular appeal. In particular, Slim Harpo's recordings of *Baby Scratch My Back* and *Rainin' In My Heart* not only made their way onto the rhythm and blues charts, but also crossed over to the pop charts. Miller's Excello recordings were cut between 1957 and 1965, with the early to mid-1960s being the heyday of what became known as the "swamp sound."

THE BLUES ROLL ON IN CHICAGO

Just as Muddy Waters and Howlin' Wolf ushered in a new sound in Chicago blues, during the mid-1950s and into the 1960s another generation of blues men emerged to shake up the blues tree. Some of these younger artists emerged from Muddy's band or had played with the Wolf, and others were a new generation of southern, mostly Mississippi, migrants who made their way to Chicago.

Among the players who emerged from the earlier generation of bands were harmonica players James Cotton, Little Walter, and Junior Wells, Muddy's ace pianist Otis Spann, and guitarists Hubert Sumlin, Jimmy Rogers, and Buddy Guy. Many of these artists had some influence, but never established the clear identity and image that Waters and Wolf put across in their performances and recordings. Buddy Guy is the exception to this rule, but his career has taken off only during the last 10 years. He had served as a studio guitarist at Chess Records, and he was not taken seriously as a solo artist for some years.

Another group of artists established careers as bandleaders without serving an apprenticeship with the existing blues masters. These artists included two Robert Johnson protégés: his stepson, Robert Jr. Lockwood, and Johnson's sometime traveling partner Johnny Shines. Shines performed in the traditional Delta style, but Robert Jr. was a very jazz-oriented performer who numbered among his influences Kenny Burrell, George Benson, and Wes Montgomery. Many of the other emerging guitarists were more rock and soul oriented. This new generation played solid-body electric guitarists, rather than the acoustic guitars with pick-ups favored by the older generation, including Muddy Waters.

We previously mentioned that Elmore James was the artist who took the slide sound and revved it up to the electric blues levels favored by rock and rollers. His version of Robert Johnson's *Dust My Broom*, which Elmore recorded on various labels at different times, became the anthem of slide guitarists during the 1960s. Other blues artists of the younger generation included Luther Allison, J.B. Hutto, Albert Collins, Johnny Copeland, Hound Dog Taylor, Freddie King, Magic Sam, Otis Rush, and Ko Ko Taylor, the "queen of the blues." These artists tended to fall into one of two categories. One group played slide guitar, and usually played with their right-hand fingers, with or without finger picks. The other faction were influenced by B.B. King, and usually played with a flat pick and used many string bends in the left hand.

By the 1960s, both the finger-style and flatpick guitarists tended to play fairly loud electric guitar, using solid-body guitars and larger and more powerful amplifiers. This was music that worked in the rough South Side clubs; it was suitable for dancing to, and it was closer to the rhythm and blues sound that was sweeping America. It also intrigued the younger rock and roll audience — the intensity and volume of the music shared these qualities with rock and roll.

Although Jimmy Reed may not have been either the most artistic or intense blues artist, he enjoyed great success in both the pop and R&B markets with such songs as *Big Boss Man, Ain't That Lovin' You Baby, Bright Lights, Big City*, and other songs that were mostly his own compositions. Reed played guitar and harmonica at the same time, supporting the harmonica with a homemade attachment until he was able to find a store-bought harness for the instrument that left his hands free to play the guitar. Reed's songs were simple and catchy, and most had sparse instrumentation, with Reed supported by guitarist Eddie Taylor. Unlike the other Chicago musicians, Jimmy rarely played in Chicago, but toured widely, especially in the south.

The beauty of what Reed did was its simplicity. In their book *Blues for Dummies*, authors Lonnie Brooks, Cub Koda, and Wayne Baker Brooks point out that Reed landed 12 songs on the *Billboard*

Hot 100 pop charts, and 19 songs on the R&B charts, the most successful run of any blues artist. Reed was originally rejected by Chess Records, who felt that they had their hands full with Muddy Waters and Little Walter, and Jimmy became the first artist with black-owned Vee Jay Records. According to an interview taped by Dan Forte shortly before Reed died in 1976, he received no royalties for his work, although his songs were soon recorded by such major artists as The Rolling Stones and Elvis Presley. A victim of epilepsy and alcoholism, Reed, like so many other blues artists, died poor.

B.B. KING'S CAREER AND INFLUENCE

In Chapter 4, we briefly mentioned B.B. King's first hit record, his 1949 recording of Lowell Fulson's song *Three O'Clock Blues*. All through the 1950s B.B. was playing for black audiences on the so-called chitlin' circuit of small halls, bars, and clubs. In the mid-1960s, he signed with ABC Records, and he and his manager Sid Seidenberg started a systematic campaign to break through to a wider audience. Many writers consider his 1965 album, *Live at the Regal*, to be the beginning of this breakthrough. In 1967, B.B. played at Bill Graham's club The Fillmore in San Francisco. After a brief introduction by Bill Graham, B.B. got a standing ovation from the mostly white audience, the first time this had ever happened to him.

The last step in B.B.'s rise to worldwide popularity was his 1970 pop hit, *The Thrill Is Gone*. From that day until now, B.B. has been probably the best-known living blues artist. He is featured in a public service commercial about diabetes, owns blues clubs, and continues to perform and record. Part of what fueled his breakthrough was the public tribute paid to him by British rocker Eric Clapton and American blues musicians Michael Bloomfield and Elvin Bishop. Touring with The Rolling Stones in the 1970s and some 20 years later with U2 has helped to keep his popularity fresh.

B.B.'s guitar technique is unusual and immediately recognizable to his audience. He uses a great deal of left-hand vibrato, shaking the guitar string from one fret to the next higher one, and he bends the notes with his left hand, simulating a crying sound. He does not play chords to any great extent, but uses the guitar to play single-string melody lines that comment on his strong, gospel-like vocals.

BLUES MUSIC ECONOMICS

Any survey of the blues would be incomplete without some discussion of the contractual arrangements that existed between blues artists and record companies and music publishers. There are two sorts of payments that recording artists may receive:

1. A percentage of the selling price (called a "royalty") for performing on records. This can vary from no royalty at all to 10 percent of the amount charged for the record. (Session or side musicians are usually paid a flat fee for their performances.)
2. Royalties for songwriting. This ranges from payment for the song's use on a record (called "mechanical rights") to "performance rights," governing the use of songs in public places, on radio and television, or in movies, and print rights (such as sheet music or songbooks).

The unfortunate fact is that most blues artists, and many country artists as well, received flat fees in payment for their recording work. Often, either they were not offered royalties at all, or they were given an option by their producers or by the record companies of either accepting the flat fees or getting royalty payments later. Most of the artists had no notion of what they were giving up in accepting flat fees rather than royalties. Many of them also probably felt that a bird in the hand, in the form of money, was superior to a royalty that they never expected to see anyway. Quite a few of the artists fought the system by violating their contracts and recording for as many record labels as they could. Their goal was to "take the money and run." Artists such as John Lee Hooker recorded under a half-dozen or more pseudonyms, and in many cases re-recorded the same material with minimal changes.

Fees for songwriters were equally manipulated by the system. Many of the record entrepreneurs, such as J. Mayo Williams, copyrighted the artists' songs in their own names, and gave the artist-writers a pittance of an advance. These business people often played a sort of a subcontractor role with the artists, and were not in a stable business relationship with the record companies. In other words, rather than receiving what they thought was adequate payment for their services, they simply dipped into the income stream that really belonged to the performer-songwriter.

When the British blues artists came along, they started to record enormously successful records of songs picked up from blues artists. Artists such as Eric Clapton and Led Zeppelin sold millions of copies of their recordings. Blues also started to appear on successful recordings by revival folk groups and also by the young white blues singers. Successful American rock artists also recorded songs that they had learned from recordings of blues artists. Elvis Presley, in particular, recorded a number of blues songs, including his first major hit, *That's All Right,* written by Arthur "Big Boy" Crudup. A group of relatively young blues fans-managers, including Richard Waterman, started to represent some of the older blues singers, and attempted to assert their rights to their music. Waterman described an amazing scene where he drove Crudup to New York from his Virginia home, because he had been assured that Hill & Range Music, Presley's publisher, would give Crudup a big royalty check for the sales of *That's All Right.* It turned out that Julian Aberbach, the head of the company, was not able to bring himself to sign the check, and Crudup returned to Georgia and his life of privation. Ultimately, Waterman was able to collect the money, but by that time Crudup had died, so it went to his children.

Just as many of the blues artists were, to be blunt, cheated out of their royalties, a similar situation prevailed with most of the R&B artists. Ultimately, a tax lawyer named Howell Begle met Ruth Brown, and after determining that she had not received any royalties from Atlantic Records, he was able to collect back-royalties for a number of R&B artists, and to get several of the major record companies to establish a Rhythm and Blues Foundation in order to help indigent and aging artists. Several of the companies, including Atlantic and Warner Brothers, agreed to tear up the original exploitative contracts that most of the R&B artists had signed, and to pay them a 10 percent royalty on CD reissues. Bonnie Raitt, who had recorded some major hits for Capitol Records during the mid-1980s, was able to bring her influence to bear on Capitol Records, and they also changed their royalty rates for reissue projects, and contributed to the R&B Foundation.

Many of the people who have written about the blues have emphasized the racist aspects of these exploitative relationships, but it should also be clear to the reader that some of the "bad guys" were black entrepreneurs, such as J. Mayo Williams, or black-owned record companies such as Peacock and Vee Jay. Other record company executives took a paternalistic view, preferring to give their artists expensive gifts — from cars to homes — reasoning that the artists themselves would just "waste" the money if they paid them in cash. Etta James, for one, expressed her relief that Leonard and Phil Chess bought her a home, rather than giving her money during a time when she would have squandered it on drugs. Still, the attitude of entrepreneurs such as Chess seems, in retrospect, to reflect a racist system.

Finally, the reader should be aware that even when the artists signed contracts promising them royalties, the artists seldom received anything. This was because most of the costs of making the record — the recording studio's time, money paid to studio musicians or engineers, the artwork if albums were produced, and any costs of promotion by independent record promoters — were charged against artists' royalties. Even when the artist made records that sold reasonably well, they remained in debt to the record company until all these "chargebacks" were recouped. This system still prevails today, so that even in the pop music marketplace relatively few artists really see any royalties from records. Those who write songs technically receive songwriting royalties, but some contracts specify that these royalties are also deducted from the artists' income.

Besides the issue of royalties, there is the question of actual ownership of record companies and music publishing operations. With the exception of the short-lived Black Swan label, which only lasted from 1921 to 1923, there were no black-owned companies issuing records during the heyday of the blues. Black Swan started out as a vehicle for issuing black classical music recordings, but quickly became dominated by blues records, until it was taken over by Paramount Records in 1923. The R&B and rock era of the 1950s and 1960s was notable for the absence not only of black owners, but even of many highly placed black record executives. Don Robey ran the successful Peacock Records in Houston, James Bracken and Vivian Carter operated Vee Jay in Chicago, and, of course, Berry Gordy ran the enormously popular Motown Records in Detroit. There were many smaller companies, many of which only lasted for a few years. A few of them were Bob Geddins's several labels operating out of Oakland, and a number of labels owned by Bobby

Robinson in New York City. During the 1970s Philadelphia International was an extremely important soul music label operated by Kenny Gamble and Leon Huff. Brian Ward, writing in his book *Just My Soul Responding: Rhythm and Blues, Black Consciousness and Race Relations*, lists about three dozen black-owned labels, but he also points out that there were approximately 400 to 600 labels with a strong R&B emphasis immediately after World War II, and there were something like 3000 independent record labels overall by 1960. It should be understood that even the black-owned labels did not record a whole lot in the way of pure blues. Jimmy Reed's records for Vee Jay and some other Vee Jay records by such artists as John Lee Hooker, and Bobby Robinson's occasional forays with such blues artists as Brownie McGhee, are the exceptions to the rule. Most of the other labels focused on R&B, or in Motown's case on the white teenaged market.

Henry Glover was a black record producer who worked for Syd Nathan at King Records in Cincinnati. Glover produced not only many R&B recordings, but country and western records as well. Although other black musicians or entrepreneurs such as J. Mayo Williams had worked for white-owned record companies, Glover was the first black record executive who was treated as a regular staff producer, without suffering the indignities of being treated like a second-class citizen.

Music publishing initially was an area that tended to attract trained musicians. The outstanding early black publishing company was W.C. Handy's operation, which he started after selling all rights to his lucrative *Memphis Blues*. During most of Handy's career, sheet music was considered the most lucrative aspect of music publishing. By the 1950s and 1960s royalties from airplay and from the sales of records far exceeded the value of sheet music. R&B pioneers such as Sam Cooke and Curtis Mayfield were able to start their own music publishing operations, and such record labels as Motown also owned the bulk of the publishing rights on most of their recordings.

ARTISTIC CONTROL

In addition to the financial complaints that many blues artists have against record companies, personal managers, music publishers, and booking agents, there is also the aspect of the record company wanting to control the artist's work. Otis Rush was an artist who became increasingly frustrated with the record business, as he went from one bad record deal to another. He complained about record companies attempting to influence his musical direction through their choice of record producers, musicians, and repertoire.

The record producer, in earlier days called a record company artist and repertoire(A&R) "man," could (and still can) control an artist's use of other musicians or vocalists, choose a particular studio or engineer, and pressure the artist to record particular songs, or to arrange the music in a particular way. As the technical aspect of the recording process developed, music began to be recorded on four- and eight-track recorders during the early 1960s, and had to be mixed down to a stereo recording. This process often took place after the artist was gone from the studio, so that it was the producer who often made the final choices as to how prominent certain instruments or voices should be on the final record. When this working relationship was a positive thing, as with Albert King's relationship with his producer — Booker T and The MGs drummer Al Jackson — this could lead to the expansion of an artist's musical vision. When the two parties did not see eye to eye — as in Marshall Chess's recording of Muddy Waters's album *Electric Mud*, where he attempted to update Muddy Waters's sound and repertory to reflect the rock revolution — the artist is placed in the peculiar and uncomfortable position of renouncing his own work.

Summary

The folk music revival of the late 1950s and early 1960s led to a similar awakening of interest in the blues. This was fueled by the rediscovery of important early blues artists, and through the work of white blues enthusiasts who became recording artists. British blues-rockers also contributed to expanding interest and enthusiasm in the blues, both through their own performances and by performing with such American blues artists. The R&B market also grew, thanks to an influx of gospel-influenced singers who introduced a new style, called "soul," in the early 1960s. Nonetheless, blues and R&B artists were often denied royalties and songwriting income from their work, and also did not always have control over how their music was recorded or marketed.

THE NEW GENERATION OF BLUES ARTISTS: 1980–TODAY

TIMELINE: 1980–2003

1980 *The Blues Brothers* movie released
      Ronald Reagan elected president of the United States

1983 Stevie Ray Vaughan's *Texas, Flood* album issued

1986 Bonnie Raitt's *Nick of Time* and Robert Cray's
      Strong Persuader issued, becoming pop hits

1990 Complete Robert Johnson double CD released

1991 First Gulf War began
      Bill Clinton elected president of the United States

1994 A new group of younger bluesmen appeared: Eric Bibb, Guy Davis,
      Ben Harper, Keb Mo, Otis Taylor, and Alvin Youngblood Hart

2001 September 11 bombings in the United States, followed by the United
      States action against Afghanistan

2003 Congress declared 2003 the "Year of the Blues"
      Martin Scorsese produced/directed five films on the blues for public tele-
      vision, followed by release of DVDs and CDs

THE LATE 1970s: THE BLUES HIATUS

The period starting in the mid-1970s saw the meteoric rise of punk music and disco. Soul music's popularity faded, as the slicker soul productions, such as those of Gamble and Huff in Philadelphia, lost popularity. The pop music scene was divided into two camps: on the one hand there were the technology-driven disco records, featuring synthesizers, drum machines, and samplers, and on the other hand was punk music. Disco was very much a record producer's music, and the impetus for the music was putting the beats together, getting the singer to perform the vocal, and then putting the vocal and instrumental tracks together. It was not an idiom that encouraged anything resembling blues, although the occasional record such as Trammps' *Disco Inferno* did have some R&B ingredients. Punk was sort of jointly birthed in New York and London, and was, if anything, even farther away from the blues. It was the absolute opposite to disco in that the music was ultra-simple; there was no orchestration at all, and the whole intent was that it did not require a great deal of musical sophistication to play the music. Punk soon evolved into New Wave music and even glam rock, but once again these musical genres did not have much to do with the blues.

Nonetheless, on the margins of "pop" music, there were signs of a growing revival of interest in the blues. The soulfulness of blues songs would stand in stark contrast to both the mechanical disco styles and the sometimes flippant attitude of punk. And the skill necessary to perform the music was also in solid contrast to both machine-made disco and do-it-yourself punk. Blues — broadly defined to include artists who perform a mix of traditional blues, R&B, and gospel music — would enjoy renewed popularity from the 1980s to the turn of the new millennium.

BONNIE RAITT

There are a number of artists whose careers we could have placed into different sections of this book. Bonnie Raitt's career started in the mid-1960s, when she began to study with such blues masters as Son House and Fred McDowell. She recorded nine albums for Warner Brothers in the 1970s; they varied in artistic merit, but none of them was commercially successful. Her career languished until 1986, when she signed with Capitol Records, and recorded *Nick of Time*. This and the next two, follow-up records were extremely successful, moving past the coveted platinum (one million sales) mark.

There is something really special about Bonnie Raitt's role in the blues revival. She is a strong slide guitar player, not simply a blues singer performing with men playing the accompanying instruments. She also is a proficient player of electric and acoustic guitar, and plays on her records as well as in performance. Over the years Raitt has become more of a songwriter in her own right, and in addition to performing older blues songs, she has covered songs by R&B artists and contemporary songwriters. Like Eric Clapton and The Rolling Stones, she has always been generous in crediting the sources of her inspiration. She even produced an album with classic blues singer Sippie Wallace in 1982, as well as singing with her. Raitt has also been an active supporter of the Rhythm and Blues Foundation, helping to raise money for impoverished blues and R&B artists, and pressuring record companies to pay realistic royalty rates to artists who had been badly exploited in their prime.

STEVIE RAY VAUGHAN AND THE AUSTIN BLUES SCENE

In 1975, Clifford Antone opened up his Antone's blues club in Austin, Texas. The manager was singer Angela Strehli, and she, pianist-singer Marcia Ball, and singer Lu Anne Barton became a central force in the local blues scene. Antone started a record label in 1986, and he has recorded Barton, Ball, and Strehli, and more recently Sue Foley, a powerful guitarist and singer.

Two brothers were also on the scene: Jimmy and Stevie Ray Vaughan. Both had played in various local groups, with Jimmy settling in with his band, The Fabulous Thunderbirds, while younger brother Stevie Ray started his own band. *Texas Flood*, Stevie's 1983 recording on Columbia Records, became a major hit, and with Bonnie Raitt's work sparked the blues revival of the 1980s. Stevie was a dynamic guitarist who was strongly influenced by Jimi Hendrix. Like Jimi, Stevie had one foot in rock, and the other in the blues, and that seemed to help gain both of them an audience that went beyond the mainstream blues listener. Stevie went through some drug and alcohol rehabilitation problems, and just when he seemed to be coming out of the woods, he died in a helicopter crash in 1990. He was 35 years old.

INDEPENDENT LABELS FILL THE VOID

When the blues temporarily lost their steam in terms of commercial popularity during the 1970s, several independent labels arose to cater to the blues audience. Chicago blues fan Bruce Iglauer started Alligator Records in the mid-1970s, and quickly built it into the strongest of the blues independents. Iglauer recorded many of the Chicago blues artists who were without a home with the demise of Chess and Vee Jay Records in the 1970s, and the decline of the 45 rpm single. Blind Pig began in 1977 in Ann Arbor, Michigan, recording a blend of young and old black and white artists. Rounder Records in Somerville, Massachusetts, began as a small roots-oriented record company, but they experienced some unexpected success when they released an album by Wilmington, Delaware blues-rocker George Thorogood in 1977, which went gold (selling over 500,000 copies). They established themselves as the premier roots record company in the United States by issuing not only blues recordings, but many bluegrass albums. Their blues offerings range from reissues of out-of-print recordings on other labels, to a long-term relationship with Rory Block, whose career has paralleled that of Bonnie Raitt, without the significant commercial success that Raitt has enjoyed. Rounder also has recorded a number of albums in New Orleans, including Cajun and R&B artists. Currently, they are reissuing over a hundred CDs of music recorded by the late Alan Lomax, which includes a substantial helping of blues offerings.

Arhoolie Records in the San Francisco Bay area began its operations in 1960. Owner Chris Strachwitz, an Austrian immigrant, formed the company in order to release his recordings of Texas songster Mance Lipscomb. Subsequently, he has recorded a large number of blues albums, along with releasing many reissues of Mexican American music, and other roots music that he enjoys, notably Zydeco artist Clifton Chenier. Bob Koester continues to release blues albums alongside his larger jazz catalog on his Chicago Delmark label.

There is still a market for down-home, juke-joint blues, and R&B music among older African Americans, particularly in the southern United States. Malaco Records, in Jackson, Mississippi, continues to service that audience with recordings by such artists as Z.Z. Hill.

THE RETURN OF ROBERT JOHNSON

In the late 1980s, Lawrence Cohn was a record producer working at Columbia/Sony who had a great love for the blues. He was determined to release all of the Robert Johnson material in a CD box. There were many problems in putting the package together; some had to do with attempting to trace the artist's surviving relatives, and others had to do with permissions to use the two surviving pictures of Robert. (It is rumored that Mack McCormick may have other photos of Johnson, but it appears that this will not be confirmed until and unless he publishes his book about Johnson.) Cohn was able to bring all the pieces of the puzzle together, and he also enlisted some of Sony's engineers and wonderful audio equipment to attempt to clean up the sound as much as possible without destroying the energy of the original performances. Cohn felt that there was definitely a market for Johnson's work, but to make sure that he reached that market, he enlisted Eric Clapton and Keith Richards to write part of the notes that accompanied the package. To everyone's amazement, the package quickly sold over a half-million copies. With his foot planted solidly in the corporation's door, Cohn next convinced the company to reissue recordings by such artists as Brownie McGhee, Blind Boy Fuller, and Son House. Sony also put together themed anthology packages on specific subjects, such as slide guitar and good time party music. Although none of these packages did anywhere near as well as the Robert Johnson reissue, they sold well enough that RCA raided its Bluebird Record archives, and MCA went back to its Decca and Chess recordings to release a number of blues packages.

Meanwhile some of the older artists, such as Johnny Shines and Robert Jr. Lockwood, continued to tour, and more interest developed in them in particular because of their connection to Robert Johnson. In turn, these artists were interviewed by various periodicals, especially *Living Blues* magazine, which stirred up more interest. Another Delta blues artist who found a new audience was Dave "Honeyboy" Edwards, who had recorded for the Library of Congress in 1942, and had known Son House, Robert Johnson, and Charley Patton.

Many other artists emerged during this period, or they continued careers that had begun in the 1960s. Piedmont blues artist John Jackson started his recording career with Arhoolie Records in 1965 at the age of 51, and he continued to record and occasionally tour through 1999. Henry Townsend was a St. Louis bluesman who began recording in 1929, and recorded through the 1980s. John Cephas and Phil Wiggins are a guitar and harmonica duo in the Brownie McGhee and Sonny Terry tradition. They began recording together in 1982, and continue to record and to tour widely today. Their music is the Piedmont blues, mixed with some originals and a sprinkling of country and western and gospel songs. R.L. Burnside was born in 1926, but his recording career did not begin until 1992, when Jim O'Neal, former editor of *Living Blues* magazine, started his Fat Possum record company. Burnside came to O'Neal's attention through blues scholar/musician Robert Palmer's film *Deep Blues*. Burnside has recorded with white rock star Jon Spencer's Blues Explosion, and with studio musicians, as well as members of his own family. On most of his recordings, Burnside plays electric guitar, and performs the sort of music that you might hear in a Mississippi juke joint, but there are also a few recordings where he plays acoustic guitar.

THE EMERGENCE OF YOUNG, BLACK BLUES ARTISTS

Before the 1990s, there were only a handful of younger black blues artists practicing the art of the blues. Taj Mahal had been performing since the 1960s, but he was more of a sort of contemporary songster than an outright bluesman, mixing world music styles in his repertoire. There were a few lesser-known artists as well. Larry Johnson was mentioned earlier in this book as a New York City artist who had studied with both Gary Davis and Brownie McGhee, but Johnson did not tour widely and recorded only two albums between 1975 and 1989. Jerry Ricks is a Philadelphia-born blues artist who learned to play guitar while working at the Second Fret coffeehouse in Philadelphia. He hosted such visiting bluesmen as Mississippi John Hurt and Skip James, and Ricks developed an encyclopedic knowledge of blues styles. He served as road manager for a Buddy Guy/Junior Wells State Department blues tour in Africa, so he also gained considerable knowledge of Chicago blues. Ricks moved to Europe during the

1970s, and recorded a number of albums, but they were not released in the United States.

However, starting in 1994, a group of (mostly) younger, black blues artists emerged. The primary thing that distinguished them from the Chicago blues stylists was that this new group of artists made a conscious attempt to recapture blues root style, performing a combination of their own songs and songs by the older black artists like Skip James. Although a number of these artists played electric guitar, the emphasis was on acoustic music styles. This group of artists included Eric Bibb, Guy Davis, Ben Harper, Corey Harris, Alvin Youngblood Hart, Keb' Mo', and Otis Taylor. These artists were mostly from urban areas, and were well educated. Many of them had been exposed to many different musical styles, and Bibb and Davis came from families who were active in the arts, in music and theater, respectively. Bibb's father, Leon Bibb, was a classically trained musician who had achieved some popularity as a folksinger during the 1950s and 1960s. Bibb grew up around such artists as Pete Seeger and Bob Dylan, so although his recordings are centered in the blues, they include elements of gospel music and even occasional R&B songs. Eric Bibb has toured widely in Europe, and makes his home in Sweden.

Corey Harris was born in Denver, went to college in Maine, and spent time in Africa studying African languages. He has maintained an interest in the African connections with the blues through more African travel. He has also recorded songs by such older artists as Blind Lemon Jefferson, Memphis Minnie, and Son House. Of all of these musicians, Ben Harper is probably the most eclectic. His music spills over to rock sufficiently that he was able to be the opening act for the Dave Matthews Band in their summer 2000 tour. Harper is also more dedicated to songwriting and less to performing other people's songs than the majority of these artists.

Keb' Mo' has a diverse musical background, including a stint with violinist Papa John Creach's band, and a period when he was a contract songwriter. He has written many of the songs on his albums, although he has also recorded Robert Johnson's *Love In Vain*, as well as other songs written by Johnson. Of all of the younger artists, Mo's work is the most R&B oriented, and his records tend to use studio musicians, and to be slickly produced for the contemporary pop market.

Otis Taylor was born in Chicago, but has lived most of his life in the Denver area. Taylor spent a great deal of time hanging out at the Denver Folklore Center, where he was exposed to an enormous reservoir of American roots music. After a successful and lengthy stint as an antique dealer that lasted from 1977 to 1995, he resumed an interrupted musical career with tremendous energy. Like Taj Mahal, Taylor unashamedly plays banjo as well as acoustic and electric guitar. Many of his songs demonstrate social concerns about such issues as lynching, slavery, and other aspects of African American history.

It bodes well for the future of the blues that Harper and Harris are in their mid-30s, Hart is in his early 40s, Keb' Mo' is in his early 50s, and Taylor is in his mid-50s. Meanwhile Jerry Ricks returned to the United States during the 1990s, and is recording and touring. It is also significant that both Harper and Keb' Mo' have major label recording deals, which means that powerful economic forces have made an investment in these supporting contemporary blues artists.

BLACKS, WHITES, AND THE BLUES

In addition to the "new wave" of black artists playing blues music, there are a substantial number of younger white artists currently performing. This includes both men and women. However, there is a special significance to younger black musicians returning to the blues as an appropriate forum for their musical ideas. After all, the blues are an African American musical style, just as jazz or R&B are products of black musical invention. As blues have gained a white audience, a phenomenon that really started as early as the 1950s, but has accelerated over the years, there has been considerable controversy about white artists performing the blues. Some traditionalists, particularly the editors of *Living Blues* magazine, have limited their coverage of white blues artists, arguing that their work is of limited significance to the roots or development of the art form.

It is true that the earlier white blues artists tended to be slavish imitators of black blues styles, and it is also true that some of the younger white artists, whether we are talking about Paul Butterfield or The Rolling Stones, quickly achieved more popularity and much more income than many of the people whose music they were appropriating. It can be argued that many of the white artists tried to achieve some balance in this process by crediting their role models, by touring with them, or, in Bonnie Raitt's case, by helping their role models to find record deals, and even participating in the recording process. Raitt, in particular, as we have mentioned, has fought to help the older black artists gain royalties that were withheld from them either by exploitative record deals or by outright theft.

But it is not simply a question of economics or credit. The ultimate question is can white artists successfully sing the blues? There is little question that the young white revivalists were able to adopt blues styles as instrumentalists, but what about the vocal styles of the blues? The reader will need to make up his/her own mind as to these questions, but undoubtedly there have been some white artists, such as Bonnie Raitt or the young Stevie Winwood, who have been able to adapt to African American musical styles without slavishly imitating specific artists. You, the reader, can make up your own mind as to the credibility of other artists who have jumped into these deep waters.

There are different subsets of the younger white blues artists. We can divide them into those who seek to play roots music styles, the electric guitar exponents of the Chicago blues, and artists who have crossed over into the shark-filled world of rock and roll.

Let us start off by discussing some of the more acoustic-oriented roots artists. These musicians vary from practicing musicians to those who are also blues scholars and teachers, who place somewhat less emphasis on recording careers. Stefan Grossman is a contemporary of Rory Block who has probably written more blues instructional books than anyone else. An inveterate student of the blues, and as already discussed a protégé of Reverend Gary Davis, Stefan was the cofounder of Kicking Mule records, and has subsequently established Vastapol, a video company that has released rare footage of blues artists. Stefan's musical turf extends outward to ragtime and original instrumental music, much of which he has performed and recorded with the superb English acoustic guitarist John Renbourn. It is interesting, if rather odd and unfair, that there is no separate biographical listing for Grossman in the comprehensive *All Music Guide to the Blues*, a listing of virtually every blues record currently available.

Other teacher-performers include Pittsburgh's Ernie Hawkins and Andy Cohen, who currently lives in Memphis. Both were students of Gary Davis. Steve James is another teacher-performer, who now lives in Austin. He has also written numerous articles for *Acoustic Guitar*. New York native Woody Mann has also written a number of blues instruction books, as well as performing blues, ragtime, and jazz tunes, and also his own compositions. Mike Dowling is an excellent blues artist-instrumentalist from Wyoming, who has made instructional tapes and teaches blues workshops.

There are a number of blues instruction camps where students can come and study with many of these artists. Among these camps are the Port Townsend (Washington) Blues Guitar Workshop and the classes offered at Davis & Elkins College in West Virginia.

Three significant musicians who are not teachers are Sonny Landreth, Kelly Jo Phelps, and Ry Cooder. Landreth is a Louisiana guitarist and dobro player who played in Zydeco bluesman Clifton Chenier's band, and has played guitar on many recordings by other musicians, as well as recording on his own. Landreth is known for his electric slide work. Phelps plays acoustic slide guitar, and his recordings are a blend of traditional tunes, blues compositions by some of the masters, and his own tunes. He is particularly adept at setting a mood through his skilled guitar playing and moody vocals. Ry Cooder is an extremely eclectic musician, whose work has ranged from traditional blues and country music to world music styles and film scores. Cooder has maintained a 30-year relationship with Warner Brothers Records, and he has also played on numerous recording sessions, including some with The Rolling Stones. His musical forte is taking traditional songs to new dimensions by adding unexpected instrumental styles from other musical idioms. For example, he might add a Tex-Mex accordion to a traditional blues song.

WOMEN OF THE BLUES

There are many white female blues singers who continue to record and perform. Tracy Nelson, who lives near Nashville, came upon the scene at about the same time as Janis Joplin appeared. Nelson is a superb vocalist, though less spectacular, than Joplin was, and has recorded blues, country music, and even R&B and rock-tinged music during her almost 40-year recording career. Possibly her versatility has contributed to her lack of ever achieving mass appeal. Mary Flower is a singer, songwriter, guitarist, and teacher who has lived in Denver for over 30 years. She has taught at some of the summer blues workshops, and has half a dozen fine albums available. Flower is also an excellent dobro player, and a capable country-folk artist, but for some years has concentrated on performing the blues in a concert program she calls *Women of the Blues*.

Ruthie Foster is a black blues artist with a background in a variety of musical styles who is currently performing and recording. Jessie Mae Hemphill is a black blues singer and songwriter whose grandfather was a renowned flute player in the north Mississippi hill tradition. Hemphill recorded several albums in the 1980s with a small band that has the feel of early Muddy Waters records. Hemphill is 69 years old, and since suffering a stroke in 1994, she no longer performs. Other contemporary female blues artists include slide guitarist Joanne Connor, Debbie Davies, Deborah Coleman, Shemekia Copeland, Susan Tedeschi, and British artist Dana Gillespie. Denver-based Molly O'Brien is equally capable of singing country music or blues, and some of her performances lean toward jazz as well. Copeland is the daughter of blues man Johnny Copeland, and is only 24 years old. She toured with her father even as a child, and her blend of blues and soul has already won her a W.C. Handy blues award. The Saffire-Uppity Blues Women is a blues band of three women based in Virginia. Other black blues performers include long-time recording artists with strong R&B leanings Etta James and Ko Ko Taylor.

THE YOUNG TURKS: THE BLUES ROCKERS

Two of the youngest blues guitar slingers are Jonny Lang and Kenny Wayne Shepherd. They are descendants of the Stevie Ray Vaughan guitar school, with a strong B.B. King influence as well. Lang emerged from the unlikely blues country of North Dakota as a 13-year-old hot guitarist, and today — at the age of 22 — he performs songs that range from twelve-bar blues to other more pop-oriented work that has more of an R&B feel. Shepherd's recordings have even more of a rock-band feel, with thundering guitars, bass, and drums, and vocals that sit well back in the musical mix. Shepherd sings, but is not the lead vocalist in his band. Shepherd cowrites most of his material, and more than any other artist discussed in this book his albums feel as much or more like rock records than blues recordings. We can look at Shepherd as a successor to long-time rock-blues band Z.Z. Top, without their comedic sense.

The North Mississippi All Stars is a young blues-rock-roots band. Two of its members are sons of veteran Memphis blues guitarist-record producer Jim Dickinson. Their repertoire varies from covers of old blues tunes to their own originals.

ZYDECO

In a book this short it is impossible to cover every permutation of the blues, but we would be remiss not to at least to give some mention to Zydeco music. In 1755, a group of French Canadian Catholics refused to pay allegiance to the English king, and they were deported from Nova Scotia, ending up in southwest Louisiana. They maintained their cultural traditions, and some developed relationships with African American slaves. The white and mulatto groups became known as Cajuns and creoles. Their music similarly moved into two musical styles. Cajun music is a musical style somewhat akin to country music, with nasal singing, and fiddle generally playing the leads. Zydeco is a sort of blues sung in the French language with accordion as the lead instrument, and washboard as the primary rhythm instrument. This rub-board has evolved into a metal instrument worn as a vest, and played with metal picks. There are quite a few Zydeco artists, including Boozoo Chavis and Rockin' Dopsie, but the ground-breaking stylist was accordion player-vocalist Clifton Chenier. Chenier recorded and toured numerous albums from 1955 until his death in 1987, and other recordings have been released since his death. Many of Chenier's songs were covers of blues and R&B standards translated into French.

Although Cajun music and Zydeco have traditionally gone separate ways along racial lines, successful performances of the music at major folk festivals in various parts of the country inspired Dewey Balfa, a Cajun artist, to bring both musical styles to Louisiana schools. Zydeco stands out in its own right as a unique musical style, and although there are some Zydeco bands in other parts of the country, Zydeco remains a uniquely infectious music, a sort of independent branch on the blues tree.

REGIONAL MUSIC

There continues to be a market for blues among older African Americans wherever there is a substantial black population. Several books have discussed the market for blues in Houston and other Texas cities, and there are blues clubs in any city with a substantial black population. A recent article in the music trade-paper *Music and Sound Retailer* mentioned that there were over 60 venues that featured blues in the St. Louis area. Chicago remains as a sort of blues central-headquarters for Alligator and Delmark Records, with Fat Possum Records located not too far away. There are many blues clubs, ranging from Buddy Guy's to small neighborhood bars.

THE INTERNATIONAL BLUES

We have seen that the blues became an important factor in British musical culture by the early 1960s, thanks to their adoption and endorsement by English rock bands. David Dicaire's book *More Blues Singers* includes an entire section that discusses blues singers from other parts of the world. He includes biographies of Donnie Walsh, the leader of the long-established Down Child Blues Band,Han Thessink, a Dutch blues singer, J.J. Milteau, a French harmonica player, Sven Zetterberg, a Swedish blues singer, Zuchhero, an Italian blues singer, Spanish blues guitarist Javier Vargas, Yuri Naumov, the so-called "Father of Russian Blues," Silvan Zing, a Swiss boogie-woogie piano player, Australian slide guitarist David Hole, and Japanese blues singer Shun Kikuta. In addition to these musicians, there are a number of excellent British acoustic guitarists such as ragtime specialist John James and Burt Jansch, whose music ranges from blues to English and American folksongs. Thanks to Stefan Grossman's long sojourn in Europe, his transcriptions and recordings of Dutch guitarist Leo Wijnkamp Jr. should also be added to the list. Clearly, the blues have attained international stature.

CURRENT OUTLETS FOR THE BLUES

In addition to numerous blues festivals, blues clubs, concerts, and magazines that promote and publicize the blues, there are also numerous blues societies spread throughout different parts of the world. Many of these organizations issue newsletters and sponsor festivals. Some of the festivals promote traditional blues, and others branch out to include a variety of musical styles. A recent magazine listed 46 different festivals in virtually every part of the continental United States. Blues artists also can often be found at jazz and even rock festivals. Dicaire's book gives 13 pages of listings of these organizations, spread out all over the world. Living Blues Magazine publishes an extensive festival list every year.

The House of the Blues has established blues nightclubs and souvenir shops in a number of cities. Memphis's Beale Street has been revived as a center for blues performances, and Buddy Guy and B.B. King have opened their own clubs. Some of these venues may have more to do with selling tourists merchandise then the presentation of music, but nonetheless they provide blues artists with more musical outlets.

THE MARTIN SCORSESE BLUES SERIES

The blues reached a new level of attention and respect when public television showed a series of seven films in fall 2003 as part of the "Year of the Blues" celebrations. The series was spearheaded by filmmaker Martin Scorsese, who had a long-time interest in music (he directed The Band's famous *Last Waltz* concert film). Scorsese made one of the films himself, and he commissioned six other directors to focus on their own vision of what the blues are all about. The entire series is available on DVD and VHS videos, under the title *Legacy of the Blues*, and there is a separate book that can be purchased that discusses the blues. Scorsese also supervised the reissue of a number of CDs by the artists who are depicted in the films. All in all this was an extremely ambitious project, focusing more attention on the blues idiom than has ever been attempted before.

Just as Ken Burns's 10-part documentary series on jazz created controversy, so did Scorsese's blues series. Scorsese did not make Burns's mistake of trying to cover the entire subject in a chronological fashion, so critics could not really fault him for omitting key figures or styles, as they did Burns. The series had many strengths, most notably the inclusion of archival footage. Just to see Son

House, Professor Longhair, Muddy Waters, and many other artists who are no longer alive is a rare treat, especially for young blues fans who never got the opportunity to see these artists live. On the other hand, filmmakers such as Wim Wenders who attempted to "recreate" performances by bluesmen using modern actors, in footage that was deliberately shot to look "old," did little more than confuse viewers who might have thought they were seeing "the real thing."

Unlike Burns, who at least interviewed some major jazz scholars (although some faulted him for favoring certain scholars over others), there was no attempt in the Scorsese series to interview most of the major blues scholars. Gayle Wardlow in Mississippi has done a great deal of research, and has many stories to tell. Some other major scholars, including David Evans, Jeff Todd Titon, and Bruce Bastin, were simply ignored. The average person watching these videos would get the feeling that John and Alan Lomax were the only people who ever searched for blues songs and blues singers. No credit is given to the blues scholars of the early part of the twentieth century, such as Howard Odum, Guy Johnson, or Dorothy Scarborough. There is no mention of Lawrence Gellert's fascinating collection of black protest songs from the late 1930s (see Chapter 1).

If some of these scholars had been involved in an advisory capacity, than the series probably would not have virtually omitted the subject of ragtime, or ignored or slighted most of the Piedmont artists, such as Buddy Moss, Blind Willie McTell, and Barbecue Bob. There is very little about the American white blues revival outside of Chicago. Such artists as Koerner, Ray, and Glover, the Kweskin Jug Band, John Hammond Jr., and Paul Geremia are not covered. Dave Van Ronk was still alive at the time the videos were made, and could have contributed many insights into the white blues revival, and the interactions between the revivalists and the rediscovered black musicians would have made for some fascinating stories. Van Ronk was not interviewed for the series. There is very little treatment of women blues artists, and virtually none of the current women artists, such as Susan Tedeschi, Deborah Davies, and Joanne Connors, are even mentioned. Neither are the younger blues-rockers such as Jonny Lang and Kenny Wayne Shepherd discussed.

It is odd to see a video devoted to blues piano but not one that covers the numerous and fascinating blues guitar styles, which could easily have been hosted by such blues musicians as Stefan

Grossman, Woody Mann, or Steve James. Each of these performer-scholars has transcribed dozens of guitar solos by most of the blues greats. There is also no coverage of the mélange of blues harmonica styles, or blues fiddle or banjo playing, or jug bands.

Despite these faults, each film does offer something valuable to the novice and long-time blues fan. For those who plan to use the DVDs as an introduction to the world of the blues, here is a quick guide to each film.

FEEL LIKE GOING HOME (D. MARTIN SCORSESE; WRITTEN BY PETER GURALNICK)

The first of the videos is the only one that Scorsese himself directed, titled *Feel Like Going Home*. Essentially the film involves a long-term quest by young black blues artist Corey Harris, who traces the roots of the blues in the southern United States, and then goes to Africa to discuss the African roots of the music with various African musicians.

Using Harris as a narrator-guide was an interesting idea, and mixing archival footage with contemporary performances and interviews that Harris conducted both in Africa and the United States. is effective. Scorsese cleverly uses still photos and rare films to show the conditions that bred the blues, and rare performance footage by little-known blues artists. Scorsese shows stills of convicts working and singing, and there are glimpses of pioneer blues collector John Lomax at work. Leadbelly is shown in and out of jail singing his famous song *Goodnight Irene*. There are also clips from old films or photos showing Alan Lomax, John's son, on a 1941 collecting trip collaborating with several scholars from Fisk University. We see children singing, and there is footage of interviews with Son House and a 1971 film of John Lee Hooker performing.

The film is also valuable for an extended section on the fife and drum musicians of Mississippi, who were first recorded in the 1940s by Alan Lomax, and are believed to carry forward African perform-ance traditions and styles in their music. Otha Turner is shown playing the fife, and teaching his daughter Sharde how to play. African music is mixed in with the fife and drum footage to show the musical parallels. This introduces the final extended section of the film, where Harris travels to Africa to interview contemporary performers there, including singer Salif Keita, kora player Toumain Diabete, and Al Farka Toure, who comments on the influence of John Lee Hooker on his own music. The film ends with a self-conscious "modern-meets-roots" music duet between Harris and Otha Turner performing Little Walter's big R&B hit *My Babe*.

There are times when the viewer's attention is fragmented because the film attempts to view such a broad slice of history in its two-hour framework. It would have been interesting to know how Harris himself feels that his music relates to African musical styles, and whether any of the younger black blues artists have attempted to explore African musical styles. We also might wonder whether there are any performers in Africa who are trying to play the blues, or to consciously integrate blues styles into their performances. Clearly, elements of rap and R&B styles have been incorporated into contemporary African pop music. This particular film pretty much limits its view of the blues to Mississippi blues styles, which is something of a limitation of the entire series. However, it gives the viewer an opportunity to glimpse the oppressive environment in which the blues emerged, and an opportunity to see performers who previously could only be read about in books, or listened to on records.

THE SOUL OF A MAN (D. AND WRITTEN BY WIM WENDERS)

Wim Wenders is a filmmaker who has had previous experience with music documentaries, with his prize-winning film about the Cuban Buena Vista Social Club. His video differs greatly from any of the others in this series, in that it is much more impressionistic than necessarily factual. Wenders chooses to focus his film on three blues men, holy blues performer Blind Willie Johnson, mysterious Mississippi bluesman Skip James, and the relatively obscure post-World War II musician J.B. Lenoir. Wenders also used the recognizable voice of actor Lawrence Fishburne as his narrator. This provides a certain Hollywood touch to this otherwise emotive and impressionistic vision of the blues.

The film starts out with Fishburne describing the use of Johnson's recording of *Dark Was the Night* on the Voyager space shuttle, and then shows contemporary musician Marc Ribot performing his own arrangement of the song. Ribot's version is oddly modernistic, and almost grotesque. It appears that Wenders is making some sort of point about taking a raw blues-drenched piece of music into the current world of advanced guitar technique and modernistic phrasing.

Wenders proceeds to tell the stories of Johnson, James, and Lenoir, relying on "historic recreations" to portray the early lives of the first two artists. Contemporary blues performer Chris Thomas King, who gained fame for his role in the 2000 film *O Brother, Where Art Thou?*, portraying a fictional country blues musician whose life in some ways paralleled Robert Johnson's, is used to portray both Blind Willie Johnson and Skip James in footage that has been processed to appear to date from the 1920s. There is no indication in the film that these are "recreations," and some viewers might be fooled into thinking that the footage is real, particularly since, with James, actual footage of the performer made in the 1960s follows the recreated footage.

Wenders's film also suffers from a rather odd selection of contemporary performers who are enlisted to cover the songs of Johnson, James, and Lenoir. The artists who cover James's material are put at a distinct disadvantage, because their performances often follow the (far superior) original version by James himself. Thus, we go from Skip James singing *Hard Time Killing Floor* to a rather tortured performance of the same song by contemporary singer-songwriter Lucinda Williams. Similarly, Skip performs *Illinois Blues*, and then we get Alvin Youngblood Hart's version of the same tune. From there we suddenly see Bonnie Raitt performing *Devil Got My Woman*. It is interesting that of all the younger performers recreating old blues in this video, Raitt is the only one who seems to be comfortable enough with her own vocals that she does not need to utilize exaggerated performing mannerisms, neither pushing her own vocals, nor playing exaggerated and overly busy guitar parts. The same cannot be said for the Jon Spencer Blues Explosion, who perform the same song with noisy, busy guitar and growling and loud vocals that are somewhat grotesque. The alternative-punk-folk artist Beck then delivers his own odd version of Skip's *I'm So Glad*, featuring his distorted guitar licks and toneless harmonica work. The segment on Skip James ends with audio of his interesting piano work on his *32-20 Blues*.

One of the most valuable parts of Wenders' film, and one of the most interesting portions of the seven videos, is the re-creation of the work of J.B. Lenoir. Lenoir was a Chicago-based bluesman who initially utilized trick guitar playing and zebra-striped outfits, but who became seriously involved in the Civil Rights and antiwar movements, writing songs about lynchings, Korea, Vietnam, and Eisenhower. Somehow Wenders discovered two technically rough films made about Lenoir by two young filmmakers, Steve and Ronnog Seaborg. They made a color film, hoping to get it on Swedish TV, but they were told to come back with black-and-white footage. They did so, but their work was rejected because it was considered too raw from a filmmaker's point of view. These films have never been shown before, but Wenders incorporates them into his film, along with some footage of interviews with the couple.

Lenoir was more popular in Europe than in the United States, where his political songs did not get any radio airplay and were not promoted by record companies. As is Wenders's custom throughout his film, he interpolates various current performances into Lenoir's work, including a song by John Mayall called *The Death of J.B. Lenoir*. Lenoir died in an automobile accident just at the point where it appeared that his career might begin to achieve some success.

Wenders's film is probably the most ambitious of the seven works, and by introducing us to three relatively obscure blues artists he makes a significant contribution to blues history. The use of the actors, and the variety of young performers making not-too-successful attempts to recreate the works of these three musicians only serve to remind us of how much blues history has been lost or overlooked in our current enthusiasm for the blues.

THE ROAD TO MEMPHIS (D. RICHARD PIERCE; WRITTEN BY ROBERT GORDON)

This film mostly focuses on two musicians who are at very different career plateaus, Bobby Rush and B.B. King. Rush is one of the many musicians who is carving out a living, traveling by bus with his band and back-up singers to relatively small venues in various parts of the country. For the blues fan or viewer who has a romantic impression of the life of the touring blues musician, watching Rush and his band grab whatever sleep they can on the bus, speed into the various clubs that they play, and set up and start to play will provide a good education in the life of the blues musician. Bobby dreams of "crossing over," finding the record or the one magical performance that will take his music to more than the chitlin' circuit of small and medium-sized black clubs. There is a wonderful moment in the film where Bobby Rush's bus stops, and a rather scraggly white performer sitting out on the highway exchanges guitar licks with Bobby, who gives the performer some money and his best wishes. It turns out that Bobby is 67 years old, and we get the strong sense that his life in the chitlin' circuit will never turn into the sort of success that B.B. King has enjoyed.

In contrast, we observe the career of B.B. King. B.B. had his own go-rounds with the chitlin' circuit, but he has attained a worldwide audience that transcends any one racial group or economic class. B.B. is seen recounting his earliest days, arriving in Memphis from Mississippi, and not even having fare to take the local bus, through his introduction to the rock world from his first performances at Bill Graham's Filmore West, to his years of great recording and touring success.

Intertwined with the stories of King and Rush we are taken into the world of various Memphis musicians, including pianist Roscoe Gordon, singer-DJ-personality Rufus Thomas, guitarist Calvin Newborn, and blues artist Little Milton. They tell the story of how local radio station WDIA played a key role in the 1950s and 1960s Civil Rights movement, and became a voice for black Americans well beyond Memphis itself. Others interviewed in Pierce's film include Sam Phillips, the founder of Sun Records and the man who discovered Elvis Prestey, Johnny Cash, Jerry Lewis, Charley Rich, and Carl Perkins. Sam is shown greeting Ike Turner, and they reminisce about the blues, with Sam describing how before he got involved with rockabilly music he recorded such blues artists as Howlin' Wolf and Junior Parker. Ike remarks that he never felt any sort of racial tension at Sun Studios, and Sam muses at how all of his associates shook their heads at his association with black musicians and artists. Pierce also interviews legendary white record producer-musician Jim Dickinson, who talks about his fascination with black music.

Pierce's film may lack some of the drama of Wenders's impressionistic renderings of the lives of bluesmen, but it gives us an accurate picture of what it is like to perform as a blues musician on the contemporary chitlin' circuit of small clubs.

WARMING BY THE DEVIL'S FIRE (D. AND WRITTEN BY CHARLES BURNETT)

The fourth video in the series returns to the more novelistic approach that was used by Wim Wenders. African American filmmaker Charles Burnett traveled from his California home to Louisiana as a teenager in 1955 to visit, roughly at the same time that a young man named Emmett Till came to Mississippi from Chicago. Till was lynched, supposedly for whistling at a white girl, and this film is a loose semiautobiographical creation of what Burnett experienced on his maiden voyage to the southern United States.

Burnett portrays himself as a young, naïve, somewhat puritanical preteen boy who visits his blues-singing uncle Buddy Taylor. Buddy's house is festooned with old blues posters, and his house is filled with old blues recordings. Other than that, Buddy seems to have few material possessions and no permanent personal attachments. He pursues the sort of stereotypical life of the blues man, with many women friends. All of this comes as a bit of a shock to the young boy, whose family is religious and middle class, and disapproves of Uncle Buddy's lifestyle.

It turns out that Buddy is writing a book about the blues, and this provides a framework for showing historical performances by a wide range of blues artists, including holy blues songster Gary Davis, the gentle style of Mississippi John Hurt, the jug-band-influenced performance of Sam Chatmon playing the Mississippi Sheik's big hit *Sittin' on Top of the World*, and the more modern work of T-Bone Walker, Muddy Waters, Bessie Smith, and Billie Holiday. Oddly, a clip of Skip James performing in the 1960s, also used in the Scorsese film, shows up again here. Other performance footage includes North Carolina blues guitarist-songwriter Elizabeth Cotton recalling her career as a maid, being paid 75 cents a month, then getting a raise all the way to a dollar. She talks about saving up her money and buying a guitar through a catalog for

3 dollars and 75 cents. Also shown are clips of Son House, Brownie McGhee, John Lee Hooker, and Willie Dixon.

As part of his "education" of his nephew in the ways of the blues, Buddy takes him to Dockery's Plantation, where Charley Patton lived, and to the famous crossroads where Tommy Johnson was said to have made a deal with the devil, exchanging his soul for musical skills. The story ends when Buddy takes his nephew to a rough juke joint, and the young boy is rescued by his family and returned home. Narrating the film as an adult, Burnett says how much he learned on the trip, and recounts that Buddy, like many blues men before him, became a preacher.

Burnett's film includes examples of more blues styles than are found in any of the other films. We do not know how much of the story is literally true, but along the way we have found out quite a bit about the blues.

GODFATHERS AND SONS (D. MARK LEVIN)

This film differs in many ways from the others in the Legacy series. It concentrates heavily on Chess Records, and the Chicago blues scene. As with the Memphis film, there is a key figure in the film. In this instance it is Marshall Chess, son of Leonard Chess, who founded Chess Records with his brother Phil.

Chess was an amazing company, and it recorded a large number of significant blues figures, including Muddy Waters, Howling Wolf, Little Walter, and in more of a pop vein, Bo Diddley and Chuck Berry. However, you would never know from this film that Vee Jay, one of their main Windy City competitors, was also active and involved in recording such other towering blues artists as Jimmy Reed and John Lee Hooker. More than any of the other films, this one seemed to virtually serve as a public relations piece for a single person, Marshall Chess. In the course of the film he justifies his bizarre experiments in integrating electric psychedelic rock with the blues in his *Electric Mud* recording of Muddy Waters, and a similar project that he did with Howlin' Wolf. This is done by placing rapper Chuck D. in a central role in the film as a sort of blues protégé and confidant of Marshall's. Chuck D. tells us that a band-mate of his turned him on to *Electric Mud*, which in turn led him back to Muddy's earlier work. Chuck claims that if not for this album, he would have never gone back to look at more roots-oriented blues.

Chess was notorious for not paying proper royalties, not only in its recording operation, but in its publishing company, Arc Music. Although the film pays tribute to Muddy Waters and Willie Dixon, it overlooks key facts such as Dixon's having to sue Chess in order to get his copyrights back. It is hardly surprising that Marshall Chess would defend the business practices of his father and uncle, but one would have expected Levin to have at least talked to some of the Chess artists, such as Buddy Guy, who certainly would have offered a different perspective.

Having said all of that, the film offers quite a few performances by prominent Chicago blues artists, including Ko Ko Taylor. Marshall takes us on a tour of Maxwell Street, the market where Jewish merchants sold their wares on Sunday, while the blues men played for tips on the street. Maxwell Street is basically a deserted area today. The film also includes some footage of underrated and little-known blues artist Otis Rush, and contemporary artist Lonnie Brooks. There are some shots of the two Chess Records buildings and studios, and some footage of Bo Diddley and Howlin' Wolf.

However, there are many early Chicago artists who are not covered in any detail in this film, including Tampa Red, T.A. Dorsey, Big Bill Broonzy, Washboard Sam, and Jazz Gillum. And somehow Memphis Minnie did not make it into either the Chicago or Memphis films. Tampa, Big Bill, and Minnie all recorded dozens of records, so it is difficult to see how they got overlooked.

Godfathers and Sons is possibly the weakest of all the Scorsese films, because it does not present a balanced view, and because it omits so many of the significant blues figures in Chicago, in both the artistic and business end of the blues.

RED, WHITE AND BLUES (D. MIKE FIGGIS)

Unlike *Godfathers and Sons'* one-sided depiction of the Chicago blues world, *Red, White and Blues* gives an excellent overview of the British blues revival. It describes how it all started, and developed, and there are filmed interviews and a number of performances by such major British artists as Van Morrison, Stevie Winwood, Jeff Beck, Peter Green, Eric Clapton, John Mayall, and

Mick Fleetwood. There are also some pretty credible performances by Tom Jones, whom most blues fans would not identify as someone with a strong taste for the blues.

Director Mike Figgus traces British interest in the blues to the traditional jazz bands of Humphrey Littleton and Chris Barber, and the emergence of skiffle through Lonnie Donegan's performances with Barber. Another major influence on British blues were the early tours by Big Bill Broonzy, who seems to have presented himself as an "authentic" Mississippi bluesman, rather than the hybrid, sophisticated Chicago-based musician that he really was. Other touring Americans included blues artists John Lee Hooker, Muddy Waters, and Jimmy Witherspoon. Eric Burden, the lead singer of The Animals, tells about his awe at seeing Muddy Waters. An interview with Mick Fleetwood of Fleetwood Mac, originally a blues band, tells about his experience working in pickup bands accompanying touring musicians such as John Lee Hooker. Fleetwood points out that many of the touring bluesmen would change their rhythms during different sections of a song, "and they were usually right." Another visiting American bluesman was Sonny Boy Williamson, who actually toured and recorded with The Yardbirds.

Figgus interviews virtually everyone who was involved in the English blues and R&B scenes, including Chris Farlowe, who recalls playing at the Flamingo Jazz Club, which featured late night jam sessions, and Sunday afternoon sessions as well. Farlowe's proudest moment was his record of *Bad Penny Blues*, recorded under the pseudonym Little Joe Cook. Eric Clapton, Stevie Winwood, and Albert Lee exchange reminiscences about their first guitars, and their enthusiasm for listening to and touring with the authentic American blues artists. In a heartfelt interview, B.B. King pays tribute to the British blues artists, saying they made it possible for him to appear in many places that he never would have been able to access without their help.

Toward the end there is a fine performance by Lulu, whom most Americans would regard as a straight pop singer. It seems that in England the lines between musical styles are not as strict as they are in the United States, so that Tom Jones, known in America as a Las Vegas sex symbol, is at home singing the blues. Even some of the biggest British rock stars, such as The Beatles, The Rolling

Stones, and Stevie Winwood, had a reverence for the blues; as Winwood says in the film, "we wanted to show what a wonderful kind of music it was." B.B. King has the last word, thanking British musicians for "opening doors I don't think would have been opened."

Figgus has put together an excellent history of the British blues revival. It is interesting that none of the other six films, all concerned with American music, includes nterviews with major American rock figures talking about the influence of the blues on their work. I have to wonder whether this is because the filmmakers did not think to do this, or whether the major American rock musicians were unwilling to donate their services for little or no time for financial reward. It would certainly appear that something could have been learned by interviewing such blues-based musicians as Bob Dylan, Jorma Kaukonen of Jefferson Airplane, Steve Miller, or Steven Stills.

PIANO BLUES (D. CLINT EASTWOOD)

Many Americans are probably unaware that actor–director Clint Eastwood is a good semiprofessional piano player with an enthusiastic interest in jazz. In Eastwood's film *Piano Blues*, Ray Charles serves as the central figure around whom the history of blues piano is laid out. The film opens with some footage of Ray performing *What'd I Say?*, and moves back in time to present old footage of Pete Johnson, Martha Davis, and Dorothy Donegan. We go back and forth between Ray Charles talking to Eastwood and performances by Big Joe Turner and Duke Ellington. Ray talks about listening to the Grand Ole Opry when he was a kid, and the influence of R&B pianist Charles Brown.

Eastwood has a more eclectic taste than most of the directors of this series, and blues enthusiasts will probably be a bit stunned to see Dave Brubeck, for example. Brubeck has never especially been noted as a blues roots pianist, but Eastwood is using the word "blues" in a more generic sense to encompass the jazz blues, with its more sophisticated harmonies and rhythms. Interestingly, both Brubeck and Charles regard Art Tatum, an extremely proficient jazz player with only thin blues roots, as a major influence. Ray also acknowledges the influence of early Nat "King" Cole, when Cole was playing the piano as much or more than singing.

Some of the most interesting footage in this film shows Dr. John playing piano in the style of some of his early heroes, like Champion Jack Dupree and Professor Longhair. This is intercut with some excellent film of Professor Longhair performing his composition *Tipitina*. Next comes an interview in which Texas pianist Marcia Ball reveals that her grandmother and aunt both played piano, and she also performs some examples of blues piano styles. Eastwood goes back and forth between Ball, Dr. John, and Professor Longhair, ending up in a conversation with Pinetop Perkins. Perkins talks about the Chicago blues, and his days with Muddy Waters and the influence of Waters's pianist Otis Spann.

The wide-ranging cast of pianists continues with performances and interviews with swing bandleader Jay McShann, studio musician Pete Jolly (whose highly technical, quite musical, but not especially blues-laden performances seem out of place here), jazz pianist Oscar Peterson (an Art Tatum discipline), and Fats Domino. It all ends with Ray Charles performing *America the Beautiful* with a large orchestra.

The strongest part of Eastwood's film is his obvious affection for good piano playing. It might have been useful to omit some of the more jazz-oriented players, and to have included Jimmy Yancey, the great Chicago blues pianist, and some other important musicians such as Little Brother Montgomery or Roosevelt Sykes. Once again, the value of the video lies in the footage of some significant historical figures, some of whom are no longer alive, or active.

Summary

After a decline of interest in the blues in the mid-1970s, the blues returned thanks to such performers as Stevie Ray Vaughan and Bonnie Rait, who achieved widespread popularity in the mid-1980s, sparking yet another blues revival. The mid-1990s saw the blues revitalized by an infusion of younger black artists. These developments have been followed by an ever-increasing number of younger white blues artists, including quite a few women.

In 2002, the United States Congress declared 2003 to be the "Year of the Blues." Martin Scorsese produced seven made-for-TV movies about the blues, National Public radio featured a series of programs devoted to the blues, and many books and CDs were issued or reissued. As long as the musicians who perform the blues can maintain their emotional connection to the music, alongside a knowledge of its roots, the blues will roll on.

The emergence of a younger group of black blues performers in the 1990s gives us some confidence that, although the blues will inevitably go through some musical changes, the meaning and emotion inherent in the blues will continue long after the social and economic conditions that gave rise to the music are only a distant and unpleasant memory.

APPENDIX

NOTE

In a book of this size, we have unfortunately had to omit many fine artists or to cover some important figures with very little detail. Veteran blues artists Lonnie Mack and Delbert McClinton deserve better. There are also significant idiosyncratic artists like jazz-blues artist Mose Allison or Louisiana blues singer Robert Pete Williams who have not been discussed here. It was also impossible in a book this size to list the large number of current Chicago blues artists. Another interesting subject is the large number of blind streetsingers who helped to spread the music. Fortunately many books, CDs, and videos are available to help the reader searching for more information about the blues.

BIBLIOGRAPHY

Social Histories

If you are looking for a single book to introduce you the cultural backgrounds of the blues, Levine's book is a good start.

Abrahams, Roger. (1992) *Singing the Master: The Emergence of African American Culture in the Plantation South*. New York, Pantheon.

Cobb, James C. (1992) *The Most Southern Place on Earth*. New York, Oxford University Press.

Levine, Lawrence W. (1979) *Black Culture and Black Consciousness*. New York, Oxford University Press.

Lemann, Nicholas. (1994) *The Promised Land: the Great Migration and How It Changed America*. New York, Alfred Knopf.

Lipsitz, George. (1998) *The Possessive Investment In Whiteness: How White People Profit From Identity Politics*. Phladelphia, PA, Temple University Press.

Murray, Albert. (1996) *The Blue Devils of Nada: A Contemporary America Approach to Aesthetic Statement*. New York, Pantheon.

Talley, Thomas. (1922) *Negro Folk Rhymes*. New York, Macmillan.

Woods, Clyde. (1998) *Development Arrested: The Blues And Plantation Power In The Mississippi Delta*. London, Verso.

The Blues and Africa

Charters, Samuel B. (1991) *The Roots of the Blues: An African Search*. New York: Da Capo Press.

Kubik, Gerhard. (1999) *Africa and the Blues*. Jackson, MS, University Press of Mississippi.

Oliver, Paul. (2001) *Savannah syncopators; African retentions in blues*. Reprint of 1970 book, with a new afterword in *Yonder Come the Blues*.

The Minstrel Period

Bean, Annemarie, Hatchm, James V., and McNamara, Brooks, Ed. *Inside The Minstrel Mask; Readings in Nineteenth Century Blackface Minstrelsy*. Hanover, Wesleyan University Press.

Cockrell, Dale. (1997) *Demons of Disorder: Early Blackface Minstrels and Their World*. Cambridge, U.K., Cambridge University Press.

Lott, Eric. (1993) *Love and Theft: Blackface Minstrelsy and the American Working Class*. New York, Oxford University Press.

Nathan, Hans. (1962) *Dan Emmett and the Rise of Early Negro Minstrelsy*. Norman, OK, University of Oklahoma Press.

Toll, Robert C. (1974) *Blacking Up: the Minstrel Show in Nineteenth Century America*. New York, Oxford University Press.

Ragtime

Berlin, Edward A. (1980) *Ragtime: A Musical and Cultural History*. Berkeley, CA, University of California Press.

Blesh, Rudi and Janis, Harriet. (1971) *They All Played Ragtime*. New York, Oak Publications, 1971.

Schaefer, William J. and Johannes Reidel. (1973) *The Art of Ragtime*. Baton Rouge, LA, Louisiana State University Press.

Social and Musical Background of the Blues

Allen, William Francis, Charles Pickard Ware, Lucy McKim Garrison. (1867) *Slave Songs of the United States*. New York, Peter Smith, 1951 reprint.

Carney, George, Ed. (1994) *The Sounds of People & Places: A Geography Of American Folk And Popular Music*. Lanham, MD., Rowman & Litlefield, 3rd ed.

Cohn, Lawrence. (1993) *Nothing But the Blues*. New York, Abbeville.

Conway, Cecilia. (1995) *African Banjo Echoes in Appalachia: A Study of Folk Traditions*. Knoxville, TN, University of Tennessee Press.

Cook, Bruce. (1973) *Listen To The Blues*. New York, Charles Scribners Sons.

Courlander, Harold. (1963) *Negro Folk Music U.S.A.* New York, Columbia University Press.

Dundes, Alan, Ed. (1973) *Mother Wit from the Laughing Barrel: Readings in the Interpretation of Afro-American Folklore*. Englewood Cliffs, NJ, Prentice-Hall.

Epstein, Dena J. (1977) *Sinful Tunes and Spirituals*. Urbana, IL, University of Illinois Press.

Finn, Julio. (1986) *The Bluesman*. London, Quartet Books.

Floyd, Samuel. (1995) *The Power of Black Music*. New York, Oxford University Press.

Foster, Pamela E. (1998) *My Country; the African Diaspora's Country Music Heritage*. Nashville, TN self-published.

Garan, Paul. (1979) *Blues And The Poetic Spirit*. New York, Da Capo Press.

Guralnick, Peter, Santelli Robert, George-Warren, Holly and Farley, Christopher John, Ed. (2003) *Martin Scorsese Presents The Blues; A Musical Journey, the companion books to the PBS series*. New York, Amistad/Harper Collins.

Harris, Michael W. (1992) *The Rise of Holy Blues: The Music of Thomas Andrew Dorsey in The Urban Church*. New York, Oxford University Press.

Jackson, Bruce. (1972) *Wake Up Dead Man*. Cambridge, MA, Harvard University Press.

James, Willis Lawrence. (1995) *Stars in De Elements: A Study of Negro Folk Music by Willis Laurence James*. Durham, NG Duke University Press (an unpublished manuscript edited by Jon Michael Spencer).

Jones, Leroi (Amiri Baraka.) (2002) *Blues People: Negro Music In White America*. New York, Harper Collins Perennia

Katz, Bernard, Ed. (1969) T*he Social Implications of Early Negro Music in the United States*. New York, Arno.

Krehbiel, Henry Edward. (1972 reprint of 1915 book). *Afro-American Folk Songs; A Study in Racial and National Music*. New York, Frederick Ungar Publishing Co.

Linn, Karen. (1991) *That Half Barbaric Twang: The Banjo in American Popular Culture*. Urbana, IL, University of Illinois Press.

Lomax, John A., and Alan. (1934) *American Ballads & Folk Songs*. New York, the Macmillan Company.

Lomax, John A. and Alan.(1941) *Our Singing Country: A Second Volume of American Ballads and Folk Songs*. New York, Macmillan.

Moore, Allan, Ed. (2002) *The Cambridge Companion to Blues and Gospel Music*. Cambridge, U.K., Cambridge University Press.

Murray, Albert. (1982) *Stomping the Blues*. New York, Vintage Books.

Oakley, Giles. (1976) *The Devil's Music: A History of The Blues*. New York, Harvest/HBJ.

Odum, Howard W. (1925) *Negro Workday Songs*. Chapel Hill, NC, University of North Carolina Press.

Odum, Howard W. and Guy B. Johnson. (1926) *The Negro and His Songs*. Chapel Hill, NC, University of North Carolina Press.

Palmer, Robert. (1981) *Deep Blues*. New York, Viking Press.

Parrish, Lydia. (1942) *Slave Songs of the Georgia Sea Islands*. New York: Creative Age Press.

Patterson, Daniel W., Ed. (1991) *The Sounds of the South*. Chapel Hill, NC, Southern Folklife Collection, University of North Carolina.

Ramsey, Frederic. Jr. (1960) *Been Here And Gone*. New Brunswick, NJ, Rutgers University Press.

Sandberg, Larry and Dick Weissman. (1989) *The Folk Music Sourcebook: New, Updated Edition*. New York, Da Capo.

Scarborough, Dorothy. (1925) *On the Trail of Negro Folk-Songs*. Cambridge, Harvard University Press

Sidran, Ben. (1971) *Black Talk*. New York, Holt, Rinehart & Winston.

Southern, Eileen, Ed. (1971) *Readings In Black American Music*. New York, W.W. Norton.

Southern, Eileen. (1971) *The Music of Black Americans: A History*. New York, W.W. Norton.

Spencer, Jon Michael. (1993) *Blues and Evil*. Knoxville, TN, University of Tennessee Press.

Spencer, Jon Michael, Ed. (1992) *Sacred Music of the Secular City: From Blues to Rap*. Durham, NC, Duke University Press.

Tawa, Nicholas. (1984) *Serenading the Reluctant Eagle: American Musical Life, 1925–1945*. New York, Schirmer Books.

Tawa, Nicholas. (1990) *The Way to Tin Pan Alley: American Popular Song 1866–1910*. New York, Schirmer Books.

Tawa, Nicholas. (2000) *High-Minded and Low Down: Music in the Lives of Americans, 1800–1861*. Boston, MA, Northeastern University Press.

Tosches, Nick. (2000) *Where Dead Voices Gather*. Boston, MA, Little, Brown & Co.

Tracy, Steven C., Ed. (1999) *Write Me A Few of Your Lines; A Blues Reader*. Amherst, MA, University of Massachusetts Press.

Van Der Merwe Peter. (1989) *Origins of the Popular Style: The Antecedents of Twentieth-Century Popular Music*. New York, Oxford University Press.

Weldon, Pete and Toby Byron (1991) *Bluesland*. New York, Dutton.

White, Newman I. (1928) *American Negro Folk-Songs*. Cambridge, MA, Harvard University Press.

Classic Blues

Albertson, Chris. (2003) *Bessie,* Revised Edition, New Haven, CT, Yale University Press.

Brooks, Edward. (1982) *The Bessie Smith Companion*. Wheathampstead, U.K., Cavendish Publishing Co.

Davis, Angela (1998) *Blues Legacies and Black Feminism: Gertrude "Ma" Rainey, Bessie Smith and Billie Holiday*. New York, Pantheon Books.

Harrison, Daphne Duval. (1988) *Black Pearls: Blues Queens of the 1920's*. New Brunswick, NJ, Rutgers University Press.

Leib, Sandra. (1981) *Mother of the Blues: A Study of Ma Rainey*. Amherst, MA, University of Massachusetts Press.

Moore, Carmen. (1970) *Somebody's Angel Child: The Story of Bessie Smith*. New York, Crowell.

Stewart, Baxter Derrick. (1970) *Ma Rainey and the Classic Blues Singers*. New York, Stein & Day.

Black Country Blues

Baston, Bruce. (1971) *Crying for the Carolinas*. London, Studio Vista.

Bastin, Bruce. (1986) *Red River Blues: The Blues Tradition In The Southeast*. Urbana, IL, University of Illinois Press.

Charters, Samuel. (1975) *The Country Blues*. New York, Da Capo Press.

Charters, Samuel. (1991) *The Blues Makers*. New York, Da Capo Press.

Evans, David. (1987) *Big Road Blues: Tradition and Creativity in the Folk Blues*. New York, Da Capo Press.

Ferris, William. (1984) *Blues From The Delta*. New York, Da Capo press.

Garan, Paul and Beth. (1992) *Woman With Guitar: Memphis Minnie's Blues*. New York, Da Capo Press.

Lomax, Alan. (1993) *The Land Where The Blues Began*. New York, Pantheon Books.

Mitchell, George. (1971) *Blow My Blues Away*. Baton Rouge, LA, Louisiana State University Press.

Oliver, Paul. (1984) *Blues Off the Record: Thirty Years of Blues Commentary*. New York, Da Capo Press.

Oliver, Paul. (1989) *Screening the Blues: Aspects of the Blues Traditions*. New York, Da Capo Press.

Oliver, Paul. (1997) *The Story Of the Blues*. Boston, MA, Northeastern University Press.

Oster, Harry. (1969) *Living Country Blues*. Detroit, Folklore Associates.

Pearson, Barry Lee. (1990) *Virginia Piedmont Blues" The Lives and Art of Two Virginia Bluesmen*. Philadelphia, PA, University of Pennsylvania Press.

Titon, Jeff Todd (1994) *Early Downhome Blues: A Musical and Cultural Analysis*. 2nd ed., Chapel Hill, NC, University of North Carolina Press

Wardlow, Gayle Dean. (1998) *Chasin' That Devil Music; Searching For The Blues*. San Francisco, CA, Miller Freeman Books.

Gospel and Holy Blues

Harris, Michael W. (1992) *The Rise of Gospel Blues; The Music of Thomas Andrew Dorsey In The Urban Church*. New York, Oxford University Press.

Heilbut, Anthony. (1985) *The Gospel Sound: Good News and Bad Times*. Revised edition, New York, Limelight Editions.

Young, Alan. (1997) *Woke me Up This Morning; Black Gospel Singers and the Gospel Life*. Jackson, MS, University Press of Mississippi.

Urban Blues, Rockabilly, Rock Blues, the Folk and Blues Revivals, British Blues

Bane, Michael. (1992) *White Boy Singin' The Blues: The Black Roots of White Root*. New York, Da Capo Press.

Brunning, Bob. (1995) *Blues: The British Connection*. London, Helter Skelter Publishing.

Cantwell, Robert. (1996) *When We Were Good: The Folk Revival*. Cambridge, MA, Harvard University Press.

Dicaire, David. (1999) *Blues Singers*. Jefferson, NC, McFarland.

Escott, Colin and Martin Hawkins. (1991) *Good Rockin' Tonight: Sun*

Records and the Brith of Rock'n Roll. New York, St. Martin's Press.

Filene, Benjamin. (2000) *Romancing the Folk: Public Memory & American Roots Music*. Chapel Hill, NC, University of North Carolina Press.

Gillett, Charlie. (1983) *The Sound of The City: The Rise of Rock And Roll*. Revised and Expanded Edition, New York, Pantheon Books.

Groom, Bob. (1970) *The Blues Revival*. London, Studio Vista Books.

Gurlanick, Peter. (1981) *Feel Like Going Home: Portraits In Blues And Rock 'n Roll*. New York, Vintage Books.

Hatch, David and Stephen Millward. (1987) *From blues to rock: An Analytical History of pop music*. Manchester, U.K., Manchester University Press.

Keil Charles. (1991) *Urban Blues, With A New Afterword*. Chicago, IL, University of Chicago Press.

Obrecht, Jas, Ed. (2000) *Rollin' And Tumblin': The Postwar Blues Guitarists*. San Francisco, CA, Miller Freeman Books.

Rosenberg, Neil. V., Ed. (1993) *Transforming Tradition: Folk Music Revivals Examined*. Urbana, IL, University of Illinois Press

Protest Music

Bindas, Kenneth J., Ed. (1992) *America's Musical Pulse Popular Music in Twentieth-Century Society*. Westport, CT, Praeger.

Gellert, Lawrence. (1936) *Negro Songs of Protest*. New York, American Music League.

Gellert, Lawrence. (1939) *Me And My Captain (Chain Gang) Negro Songs of Protest*. New York, Hours Press.

Greenway John. (1953) *American Folksongs of Protest*. Philadelphia, PA, University of Pennsylvania Press.

Pratt, Ray. (1990) *Rhythm And Resistance: The Political Uses of American Popular Music*. Washington D.C., Smithsonian Institution Press.

Van Rijn, Guido. (1997) *Roosevelt's Blues: African American Blues And Gospel Songs On FDR*. Jackson, MS, University of Mississippi Press.

R&B and Soul

Deffaa, Chip. (1996) *Blue Hythms: Six Lives In Rhythm And Blues*. New York, Da Capo Press.

Djedje, Jacqueline Cogdell and Eddie S. Meadows, Eds. (1998) *California Soul: Music Of African Americans In The West*. Berkeley, CA, University of California Press.

George, Nelson. (1988) *The Death of Rhythm & Blues*. New York, Pantheon Books.

Gregory, Hugh. (1998) *The Real Rhythm and Blues*. London, Blandford.

Guillory, Monique and Richard C. Green, Eds. (1998) *Soul: Black Power, Politics and Pleasure*. New York, New York University Press.

Guralnick, Peter. (1986) *Sweet Soul Muisc: Rhythm and Blues and the Southern Dream of Freedom*. New York, Harper & Row.

Haralamos, Michael. (1975) *Right On; From Blues To Soul In Black America*. New York, Drake Publishers.

Hannusch, Jeff, a.k.a. Almost Slim (1985) *I Hear You Knockin: The Sound Of New Orleans Rhythm and Blues*. Ville Platte, LA, Swallow Publications, Inc.

Hoskyns, Barney. (1987) *Say It One Time For The Broken Hearted:The Country Side Of Southern Soul*. Glasgow, Fontana/Collins

Pruter, Robert. (1991) *Chicago Soul*. Urbana, IL, University of Illinois Press.

Shaw, Arnold. (1986) *Black Popular Music In America*. New York,Schirmer Books.

Shaw, Arnold. (1978) *Honkers and Shouters: The Golden Years Of Rhythm & Blues*. New York, Collier Books.

Ward, Brian. (1998) *Just My Soul Responding: Rhythm And Blues, Black Consciousness, And Race Relations*. Berkeley, CA, University of California Press.

Cajun, Zydeco, and Swamp Pop

Bernard, Shane K. (1996) *Swamp Pop: Cajun And Creole Rhythm And Blues*. Jakcson, MS, University Press of Mississippi.

Broven, John. (1987) *South to Louisiana: The Music of the Cajun Bayous*. Gretna, LA, Pelican Publishing Company.

Tisserand, Michael. (1998.) *The Kingdom of Zydeco*. New York, Arcade Publishing.

The Blues Today

Dicaire, David. (2002) *More Blues Singers*. Jefferson, NC, McFarland.

Nicholson, Robert. (1998) *Mississippi: The Blues Today!* London, Blandford.

Biographies and Autobiographies

Berry, Chuck. (1997) *The Autobiography*. New York, Harmony Books.

Bradford, Perry. (1965) *Born With The Blues*. New York, Oak Publications.

Broonzy, Big Bill, as told to Yannick Bruynoghe. (1964) *Big Bill Blues*. New York, Oak Publications.

Burton, Thomas G., Ed. (1981) *Tom Ashley, Sam McGee, Bukka White:Tennessee Traditional Singers*. Knoxville, TN, University of Tennessee Press.

Calt, Stephen. (1994) *I'd Rather Be The Devil: Skip James and the Blues*. New York, Da Capo Press.

Calt, Stephen and Wardlaw, Dayle Dean. (1988) *King of the Delta Blues: The Life and Music of Charley Patton*. Newton, NJ, Rock Chapel Press.

Charters, Samuel. (1972) *Robert Johnson*. New York, Oak Publications.

Chilton, John. (1994) *Let The Good Times Roll: The Story of Louis Jordan And His Music*. Ann Arbor, MI, University of Michigan Press.

Congress, Richard. (2001) *Blues Mandolin Man: The Life and Music of Yank Rachell*. Jackson, MS, University Press of Mississippi.

Dance, Helen Oakley. (1987) *Stormy Monday; The T Bone Walker Story*. Baton Rouge, LA, Louisiana State University Press.

Evans, David. (1971) *Tommy Johnson*. London, Studio Vista Books.

Fahey, John. (1970) *Charley Patton*. London, Studio Vista Books.

Garon, Paul. (1971) *The Devil's Son-in-Law; the Story of Peetie Wheatstraw And His Songs*. London, Studio Vista Books.

Garon, Paul and Beth. (1992) *Woman with a Guitar: Memphis Minnie's Blues*. New York, Da Capo Press.

Glover, Tony, Dirks, Scott, and Gaines, Ward. (2002) *Blues with a Feeling: The Little Walter Story*. New York, Routledge.

Gordon, Robert. (2002) *Can't Be Satisfied: The Life and Times of Muddy Waters*. Boston, MA, Little, Brown & Co.

Greenberg, Alan (1983). *Love in Vain*. Garden City, New York, Doubleday. (this is a play about Robert Johnson.)

Guralnick, Peter. (1992) *Searching For Robert Johnson*. New York, Dutton.

Handy, William Christopher. (1941) *Father of the Blues*. New York, The Macmillan Company.

Haskins, Jim. (1987) *Queen of the Blues: A Biography of Dinah Washington*. New York, William Morrow.

King, B.B., with David Ritz. *Blues All Around Me*. New York, Avon Books. Lipscomb, Mance, as told to and compiled by Glen Alyn. (1993.). *I Say Me for a Parable: The Oral Autobiography of Mance Lipscomb*. New York, W.W. Norton.

Lomax, John and Alan. (1936) *Negro Folk Spongs As Sung by Leadbelly*. New York, Macmillan.

Mahal, Taj and Stphen Foehr. (2002) *Taj Mahal: Autobiography of A Bluesman*. London, Sanctuary PublishingLtd.

Morton, David C., and Charles Wolfe. (1991) *DeFord Bailey: A Black Star in Early Country Music*. Knoxville, TN, University of Tennessee Press.

Murray, Charles Shaar. (2000) *Boogie Man: The Adventures of John Lee Hooker in the American Twentieth Century*. New York, St. Martin's Press.

Pearson, Barry Lee and Bill McCulloch. (2003) *Robert Johnson: Lost And Found*. Urbana, IL, University of Illinois Press.

Pegg, Bruce. (2002). *Brown Eyed Handsome Man: The Life and Hard Times of Chuck Berry*. New York, Routledge.

Sacre, Robert. (1987) *The Voice of the Deltal Charley Patton and the Mississippi Blues Tradition, Influences and Comparisons: An International Symposium*.

Lieges, Universities Liege Note: This was an international meeting, and some of the articles are written in French.

Scherman, Tony. (2000) *Backbeat: Earl Palmer's Story*. New York, Da Capo Press.

Tooze, Sandra B. (1997) *Muddy Waters: The Mojo Man*. Toronto, ECW Press.

Townsend, Henry, as told to Bill Greensmith (1999) *A Blues Life*. Urbana, IL, University of Illinois Press.

Wald, Elijah. (2004) *Escaping the Delta; Robert Johnson and the Invention Of the Blues*. New York, HarperCollins.

Wald, Elijah. (2000) *Josh White: Society Blues*. Amherst, MA, University of Massachusetts Press.

Wolfe, Charles and Lornell, Kip. (1992) *The Life and Legend of Leadbelly*. New York, Harper/Collins.

Zur Heide, Karl Gert. (1970) *Deep South Piano: The Story of Little Brother Montgomery*. London, Studio Vista.

Collections of Lyrics

Peters, Erskine, Ed. (1993.) *Lyrics of the Afro-American Spiritual: A Documentary Collection*. Westport, CT, Greenwood Press.

Sackheim, Eric. (1969) *The Blues Line: A Collection of Blues Lyrics*. New York, Grossman Publishers.

Taft, Michael. (1983) *Blues Lyric Poetry: An Anthology*. New York, Garland Publishing, Inc.

Titon, Jeff Todd, Ed. (1990) *Downhome Blues Lyrics: An Anthology From the Post-World War II Era*. Urbana, IL, University of Illinois Press, 2nd ed.

Songbooks (Words and Music)

Albertson, Chris and Gunthree Schuller, Commentary. (1975) *Bessie Smith: Empress of the Blues*. New York, Walter Kane & Son.

Handy, W.C., Ed., revised by Jerry Silverman. (1972) *Blues: an Anthology*. New York, Collier Macmillan Publishers.

No Author Listed. (1970) *Blues For Today*. New York, The Aberbach Group. Note: This odd little book contains all of Robert Johnson's songs, Credited to "Woody Payne"

No Author Listed. (1965) *Folk Blues: A Collection of over 100 Original Folk Songs*. New York, Arc Music.

No Author Listed. (1992) *She's Got The Blues: Songs Made Famous by the Great Women of Blues*. Milwaukee, WI, Hal Leonard Publishing Corp.

No Author Listed. (1995) *The Blues: Melody Line, Chords and Lyrics for Keyboard, Guitar, Vocal*. Milwaukee, WI, Hal Keonard Corp.

No author or date listed, ca. (1927) *The Paramount Book of Blues*. Port Washington, Wisconsin. The New York Recording Laboratories.

Grossman, Stefan, Hal Grossman, and Stephen Calt. (1973) *Country Blues Songbook*. New York, Oak Publications.

Oliver, Paul, Compiler. (1982) *Early Blues Songbook*. London, Wise Publications.

Shirley, Kay, Ed. (1963) *The Book of the Blues*. New York, Leeds Music Corp.

Silverman, Jerry. (1960) *Folk Blues*. New York, Macmillan.

Record Companies and the Music Business

Cashmore, Ellis. (1997) *The Black Culture Industry*. London, Routledge.

Cohodas, Nadine. (2000) *Spinning Blues into Gold: The Chess Brothers and the Legendary Chess Records*. New York, St. Martin's Press.

Kelly, Norman, Ed. (2002) *R & B, Rhythm & Business: The Political Economy of Black Music*. New York, Akashic Books.

Kennedy, Rick. (1994) *Jelly Roll, Bix And Hoagy: Gennett Studios And The Birth of Jazz*. Bloomington, University of Indiana Press.

Neal, Mark Anthony. (1999) *What the Music Said: Black Popular Music And Black Popular Culture*. New York, Routledge.

Olmsted, Tony. (2003) *Folkways Records: Moses Asch and His Encyclopedia of Sound*. New York, Routledge.

Weissman, Dick. (2003) *The Music Business: Career Opportunities & Self Defense, 3rd* Revised Edition. New York, Three Rivers Press.

Miscellaenous: Record Guides, Regional Blues, etc.

Abrahams, Roger. (1970) *Deep Down in the Jungle*. New York, Aldine, Revised edition.

Barlow, William. (1989) *Looking up at Down*. Philadelphia,PA, Temple University Press.

Bernard, Shane K. (1996) *Swamp Pop: Cajun And Creole Rhythm And Blues*. Jackson, MS, University of Mississippi Press.

Bird, Christiane. (2001) *The Da Capo Jazz And Blues Lover's Guide To The U.S.* New York, Da Capo Press.

Bogdanov, Vladimir, Chris Woodstra, Stephen Thomas, Erlewine, Eds. *All Music Guide to The Blues: The Definitive Guide To The Blues, 3rd ed.*, San Francisco,CA, Backbeat Books.

Brooks, Lonnie, Koda, Cub & Brooks, Wayne Baker. (1998) *Blues For Dummies*. Foster City, CA, IDG Books.

Cantor, Louis. (1992) *Wheelin' on Beale*. New York, Pharos Books.

Charters, Samuel. (1963) *The Poetry of the Blues*. New York, Oak Publications.

Cowley, John and Paul Oliver. (1996) *The New Blackwell Guide To Recorded Blues*. Oxford, U.K., Blackwell Publishers.

Gussow, Adam. (2002) *Seems Like Murder Here: Southern Violence And The Blues Tradition*. Chicago, IL, University of Chicago Press.

Davis, Francis. (1995) *The History Of The Blues:The Roots, The Music, The People From Charley Patton To Robert Cray*. New York, Hyperion.

Dixon, Robert, John Godrich, and Howard Rye. (1997) *Blues and Gospel Records, 1902–1943*. Oxford, U.K., Clarendon Press.

Donahue, Matthew A. (1999) *I'll Take You There; An Oral and Photographic History of the Hines Farm Blues Club*. Toledo, DH, Jive Bomb Press.

Duffy, Timothy. (1998) *Music Makers: Portraits and Songs from the Roots of America.* Athens, GA, Hill Street Press.

Ellison, Mary. (1989) *Extensions of the Blues.* New York, Riverrun Press.

Govenar, Alex. (1988) *Meeting the Blues; Interviews With Legends & Friends.* Dallas, TX, Taylor Publishing Co.

Hansen, Barry. (2000) *Rhino's Cruise Through The Blues.* San Francisco, Miller Freeman Books.

Harris, Sheldon. (1979) *Blues Who's Who.* New Rochelle, NY, Arlington House.

Hay, Fred J., Editor and Annotator. (2001) *Goin Back To Sweet Memphis; Conversations With the Blues.* Athens, GA, University of Georgia Press.

Kennedy, Rick and Randy McNutt, (1999) *Little Labels-Big Sound: Small Record Companies and the Rise of American Music.* Bloomington, IN, University of Indiana Press.

McKee, Margaret and Fred. Chisenhall, (1981) *Beale Black & Blue: Life And Music on Black America's Main Street.* Baton Rouge, LA, Louisiana State University Press.

Merrill, Hugh. (1990) *The Blues Route: From The Delta To California, A A Writer's Searches For America's Music.* New York, William Morrow and Company.

Moisala, Pirkko and Beverly Diamond, Ed. (2000) *Music And Gender.* Urbana, IL, University of Illinois Press.

Nager, Larry. (1998) *Memphis Beat: The Life and Times of America's Musical Crossroads.* New York, St. Martin's Press.

Oliver, Paul, Tony, Russell, M.W. Robert Dixon, John Godrich, and Howard Rye. (2001) *Yonder Come the Blue: the Evolution of a Genre.* Cambridge, U.K., Cambridge University Press. Note: This anthology contains three books first published in 1970, with new afterwords by the authors. The books are: Oliver's *Savannah Syncopators: African Retentions in the blues,* Russell's *Blacks, Whites and Blues,* and Dixon and Godrich's *Recording the Blues.*

Oliver, Paul. (1984) *Songsters and Saints.* Cambridge, U.K., Cambridge University Press.

Olsson, Bengt. (1970) *Memphis Blues.* London, Studio Vista.

O'Neal, Jim and Amy Vab Singel, Ed. (2002.) *The Voice of the Blues: Classic interviews from Living Blues Magazine.* New York, Routledge.

Robertson, Brian. (1996) *Little Blues Book*. Chapel Hill, NC, Algonquin Books Of Chapel Hill.

Rubin, Rachel and Jeffrey Melnick. *American Popular Music: New Approaches to the Twentieth Century* Amherst, MA, University of Massachusetts Press.

Russell, Tony. (1997) *The blues; from Robert Johnson to Robert Cray*. New York, Schirmer Books.

Santelli, Robert. (1993) *The Big Book of Blues: A Biographical Encyclopedia*. New York, Penguin Books.

Silvester, Peter. J. (1989) *A Left Hand Like God: A History of Boogie-Woogie Piano*. New York, Da Capo Press.

Tracey, Steven C. (1993) *Going to Cincinnati: A History of the Blues in The Queen City*. Urbana, IL, University of Illinois Press.

Tracy, Steven C., Ed. (1999) *Write Me A Few of Your Lines: A Blues Reader*. Amherst, MA, University of Massachusetts Press.

Wood, Roger (2003) *Down in Houston; Bayou City Blues*. Austin, TX, University of Texas Press.

Wyman, Bill. (2001) *Bill Wyman's Blues Odyssey: A Journey To Music's Heart & Soul. London*, DK.

DISCOGRAPHY

In almost all instances, we have decided to list only one recording by an artist. If you want to explore an artist in greater depth, check out the *All Music Guide to the Blues*, listed in the bibliography. The albums that have the artist's name followed by the essential in small letters, are an especially good buy. All of them are double sets, selling for a lower price than a single CD.

Do not get too attached to the categories given. They are simply an attempt to guide you. Many of the artists do not fit into one easy niche.

The best place for the blues fan to start is by acquiring the boxed set anthologies. They are often a great value, and because they usually include recordings by numerous artists, the listener can then determine the individual artists whose records they most likely will enjoy.

Boxed Sets

Anthology of American Folk Music. 84 Selections of 6 CD's, edited by Harry Smith. Folkways FP 251-253.

Blind Pig Records: 20th Anniversary Collection. BPCD 2001.

Blues Fest: Modern Blues of the 70's, 80's and 90's. Rhino 72191-3.

Box of the Blues. Sixty performances on Four CD's. Rounder 11661-2171-2. *Broke, Black & Blue.* Properbox 7.

Brunswick Records Greatest Hits. Brunswick BMD 30472, 30482, 30492.

Chicago; The Blues Today Vols. 1–3. Vanguard 79216-79218, 3 CD's.

Getting' Funky: The Birth of New Orleans R&B. Properbox 28.

Honkers and Screamers, Savoy 2234.

Robert Johnson: The Complete Recordings. Columbia C2K 46222-2 CD's.

Legends of Country Blues. The complete prewar recordings of Son House Skip James, Bukka White, Tommy Johnson, and Ishmon Bracey. JSP 7715 A-E. (5CD's)

Okeh Rhythm and Blues Box. Sony, 48912 (3 CD's).

Platinum Soul Legends, 1960–1975. WSMCD 100 (3 CD's).

*Roots 'N Blues The Retrospective (1925–1950)*Columbia/Legacy 47911-4CD's.

Sounds of the South-A Musical Journey from the Georgia Sea Islands to the Mississippi Delta Recorded in the Field by Alan Lomax Atlantic 4-82496-2.

Twentieth Century Blues. Catfish KATX 1.

White Country Blues: 1926–1938. Columbia 2CK 47406, 2 CD's.

Black Secular Music Before the Blues

A Treasury of Library of Congress Field Recordings. Rounder CD 1500.

Black Banjo Songsters Of North Carolina and Virginia. Folkways LC 9628.

Black Vocal Groups Volume 10: AlternateTakes & Remaining Titles c. 1919–1929 Document DOCD-5632.

Country Negro Jam Session: Butch Cage, Willie B. Thomas and Others Arhoolie. CD 372.

Deep River of Song Alabama: from Lullabies to Blues. Rounder 11661-1829-2.

Deep River of Song; Black Texicans; Balladeers and Songsters of the Texas Frontier. Rounder 11661-1821-2.

Deep River of Song:Georgia: I'm Gonna Make You Happy. Rounder 11661-1828-2.

Deep River of Song Virginia and the Piedmont: Minstrelsy, Work Songs and Blues. Rounder 11661-1827-2.

Etta Baker; One Dime Blues Finger-picked blues and traditional tunes. Rounder Cd 2112.

The Legendary De Ford Bailey: Country Music's First Star. Tennessee Folklore Society Records.

Field Recordings-Vol. 12: Virginia & South Carolina (1936–1940). Document DOCD-5614.

Field Recordings Vol. 13 Texas. Louisiana. Arkansas. Mississippi Florida.Alabama. Georgia. Tennessee. South Carolina. Delaware (1933–1943). Document DOCD-5621.

Field Recordings Volume 14 Texas, Alabama, Tennessee, Georgia, Kentucky. 1941 Document DOCD 5630.

Georgia String Bands (1928–1930). Document CD 3516-2.

Martin, Bogan and the Armstrong;That Old Gang of Mine Flying Fish 70003.

Minstrel Days and Blues: Dr. Souchon Recalls Early New Orleans. Night Train NTI CD 7080.

Mississippi Sheiks: Stop and Listen. Yazoo 2006.

Negro Blues and Hollers Rounder CD 1501 (Library of Congress re-issue).

Negro Prison Blues And Songs. Legacy International CD 326.

Negro Work Songs And Calls. Rounder CD 1517 (Library of Congress re-issue).

Prison Worksongs Recorded at the Louisiana State Penitentiary Arhoolie 448.

Roots of the Blues. New World Records 80252-2.

Secular Vocal Groups Vol. 4 (1926–1947). Document DOCD 5615.

Texas Field Recordings: The Complete Recored Works of Pete Harris, Smith Casey, a.o. Document DOCD 5231.

The Earliest Black String Bands Vol. 2 Dan Kildare. Document DOCD 5623.

The Earliest Black String Bands Vol. 3: The Versatile Three/Four, 1919–1920. Document DOCD-5624.

The Earliest Negro Vocal Groups Volume 5: 1911–1926 Document DOCD 5613.

Texas Black Country Dance Music: 1927–1935. Document DOCD 5162.

Things Ain't Like They Used To Be; Early American Rural Music Vols. 1 and 2. Yazoo 2028, 2029.

Joe Thompson Family Tradition. Rounder CD 2161.

Traveling Through The Jungle: Fife and Drum Band Music From The Deep South. Testament TCD 501.

Classic Blues Singers: Women of the 1920s

Better Boot That Thing: Great Women Blues Singers of the 1920's. Bluebird 66065-2.

Lucille Bogan & Walter Roland (the essential). Classic Blues CBL 200032.

Ida Cox (the essential). Classic Blues CBL 200017.

Female Blues Singers Vol. 1 1924–1932. Document DOCD 5505.

Female Country Blues Vol. 1 "The Twenties" (1924–1928). DA 3529-2.

Rosa Henderson (the essential). Classic Blues CBL 20024.

Alberta Hunter Vol. 3 1924–1927 Document DOCD 5424.

I Can't Be Satisfied; Early American Women Blues Singers-Town & Country. Vol. 1 — Country, Vol. 2 — Town. Yazoo 2026 and 2027.

Ladies of Blues, Disc 1, Disc 2, Disc 3. CRG 120029, 120039, 120031
Ma Rainey (the essential). Classic Blues CBL 200020.

Ma Rainey The Paramounts Chronologically Vols. 1 and 2. Black Swan HCD 12001 and 12002.

Bessie Smith The Collection, Vols. 1–4 CK44441.

Victoria Spivey (the essential). Classic Blues CBL 200014.

Sippie Wallace Women Be Wise. Alligator ALCD 4810.

Women Blues Singers 1928–1969. MCA MCAD2-11788.

Holy Blues

Reverend Gary Davis Complete Recorded Works 1935–1949. Document DOCD 5060.

Reverend Gary Davis If I Had My Way: Early Home Recordings. Smithsonian Folkways LC 9628.

Reverend Gary Davis: O Glory: The Apostolic Studio Sessions. Gene's CCD 9908.

The Complete Blind Willie Johnson. Columbia-Legacy C2K 52835.

Preachin' the Gospel: Holy Blues. Columbia-Legacy CK 46779.

Jug Bands

Gus Cannon's Jug Stompers. Yazoo 1082/83.

Clifford Hayes & The Louisville Jug Bands, Vol. 1 (1924–1926), Vol. 2. 1942RST Records JPCD 1501-1, 1502-2.

The Jug & Washboard Bands Vol. 2 (1928–1930). Story Blues CD 3514-2

Memphis Jug Band: Double Album. Yazoo 1067.

The Sounds of Memphis (1933–1939). Story Blues CD 3531-2.

Wild About My Lovin': Beale Street Blues 1928–1930. BMG 2451-2-R.

Piedmont Blues

Alabama Blues (1927–1930). Wolf WSE 113 CD.

Pink Anderson Carolina Blues, Vol. 1. Original Blues Classics OBCCD 504-2.

Barbecue Bob (the essential). Classic Blues CBL 200026.

Blind Blake (the essential). Classic Blues CBL 200035.

Blind Blake Georgia Bound. Catfish KATCD 129.

Bull City Red (1935–1939). Story Blues CD 3527-2.

Carolina Blues: Carl Martin (1930–1936) & Brownie McGhee (1940–1943) Wolf 114CD.

Cephas & Wiggins Cool Down. Alligator ALCD 4838.

Cephas & Wiggins Homemade. Alligator ALCD 4863. Note: Cephas & Wiggins are active touring and recording artists

Pernell Charity the Virginian. Trix 3309.

Blind Boy Fuller (the essential). Classic Blues CBL 200012.

Papa Charlie Jackson Vol. 1 1924-February 1926. Document DOCD 5087.

Jackson, John Blues and Country Dance Songs from Virginia. Arhoolie 1025.

The Complete Brownie McGhee. Columbia/Legacy C2N52933. Note: These are the "complete"recordings for Okeh and Columbia. McGhee also recorded for numerous other labels.

Blind Willie McTell Stomp Down Rider. Collectables COL 5552.

Willie Trice Blue & Ragged. Trix 3305.

Virginia Traditions Western Piedmont Blues. Global Village CD 1003.

Curley Weaver Georgia Guitar Wizard (1928–1935). Story Blues CD 3530-2.

Mississippi Delta Blues

Canned Heat Blues: Masters of the Delta Blues BMG 61047-2.

Dust My Broom: The Essential Recordings Of Mississippi Delta Blues. Indigo IGOCD.

Honeyboy Edwards Delta Bluesman. Earwig 4922 CD.

Son House.Delta Blues; The Original Library of Congress Sessions From Field Recordings 1941–1942. Biograph BCD 118 ADD.

Son House Mojo Workin' Blues. Columbia/Legacy CK 65515.

Skip James Skip's Piano Blues. Gene's GCD 9910.

Skip James The Complete 1931 Sessions. Yazoo 1072.

Robert Johnson: the Complete Recordings. Columbia C2K 46222.

Tommy Johnson Complete Recorded Works in Chronological Order (1928–1929). Document CD 5001.

Tommy McClennan The Bluebird Recordings 1939–1942. RCA 07863 67430-2.

Mississippi Country Blues by Jack Owens & Bud Spires: It Must Have Been The Devil. Testament TCD 5016.

Mississippi Masters; Early American Blues Classics 1927–35. Yazoo 2007.

Johnny Shines Standing at the Crossroads: Classic Mississippi Delta Blues Performances. Testament TCD 5022.

Johnny Shines and Robert Lockwood featuring Sunnyland Slim on piano. Paula PCD-14.

The Complete Plantation Recordings of Muddy Waters; the Historic 1941–2. Library of Congress Field Recordings. Chess MCA CHD 9344.

The Complete Bukka White. Columbia/Legacy CK 52782.

Robert Wilkins The Original Rolling Stone. Yazoo 1077.

Texas Blues

Black Ace: I'm The Boss Card in Your Hand. Arhoolie CD 374.

Texas Alexander Vol. 1 11 August 1927 to 15 November 1928. Matchbox MBCD 2001.

Albert Collins Ice Pickin'. Alligator AL 4713.

Johnny Copeland Bringing It All Back Home. Rounder 2050.

Blind Lemon Jefferson: The Complete 94 Classic Sides Remastered. (4CD's) JSP 7706.

Lightnin' Hopkins: All The Classics 1946–1951. 5CD's JSP 7705.

L'il Son Jackson L'il Son Jackson. Arhoolie F 1004.

Alex Moore Alex Moore. Arhoolie 1008.

Thomas Shaw; Born in Texas. Testament TCD 5027.

Texas Blues: Bill Quinn's Gold Star Recordings. Arhoolie 352.

Henry Thomas The Complete Recordings 1927–1929. Yazoo CD 1080/81.

Songsters

Libba Cotton Negro Folk Songs and Tunes. Folkways FD 3526.
Jesse Fuller the Lone Car Sings And Plays Jazz, Folk Songs, Spirituals & Blues. Good Time Jazz OBCCD 526-2 (510039).

Mississippi John Hurt Avalon Blues; Complete 1928 Okeh Recordings. Columbia/Legacy CK 64986.

Furry Lewis In His Prime (1927–28). Yazoo CD-1050.

Leadbelly Bourgeois Blues. Smithsonian Folkways SF CD 40045.

Mance Lipscomb Captain, Captain!. Arhoolie CD 465.

Leslie Riddle Step by Step Lesley Riddle Meets the Carter Family: Blues, Country and Sacred Songs. Rounder CD 0299.

White Country Blues

The Essential Sam & Kirk Magee Collection. Grand Avenue GAR 7004-2.

Hlllbilly Boogie. Columbia/Legacy CK 53490.

Emmett Miller; the Minstrel Man From Georgia. Columbia/Legacy CK 66999.

The Best of Jerry Reed. RCA 54109-2B. Note: Many country artists, like mountain musicians Dock Boggs or Roscoe Holcomb, would occasionally record blues.

Urban Blues of the 1930s

Kokomo Arnold (the essential). Classic Blues CBL 20023.

The Virtuoso Guitar of Scrapper Blackwell. Yazoo 1019.

Big Bill Broonzy Do That Guitar Rag 1928–1935. Yazoo 1035.

Big Bill Broonzy Good Time Tonight. Columbia CK 46219.

Leroy Carr Hurry Down Sunshine; The Essential Recordings of Leroy Carr. Indigo IGOCD 2016.

Cincinnati Blues. Catfish KATCD 186.

Walter Davis (the essential). Classic Blues CBL 200016.

Goergia Tom Dorsey (the essential). Classic Blues CBL 200034.

Jimmie Gordon (1934–1941). Story Blues CD 3510-2.

Merline Johnson "The Yas-Yas Girl" 1937–1941. Wolf Bob 13CD.

The Best of Big Maceo: The King of Chicago Blues Piano. Arhoolie CD 7009.

Memphis Minnie (the essential). Blues Classics CBL 200001.

Little Brother Montgomery At Home. Earwig 4918.

St. Louis Girls (1929–1937). Story Blues CD 3536-2.

Roosevelt Sykes (the essential). Classic Blues CBL 200010.

Tampa Red; the Bluebird Recordings. 1936–1938. RCA 07863 66722-2.

Tampa Red the Guitar Wizard. Columbia/Legacy CK 53235.

Henry Townsend "Mule." Nighthawk NHCD-202.

Casey Bill Weldon Guitar Swing. Catfish KATCD 217.

Peetie Wheatstraw The Devil's Son-in-Law. B.of B. 8.

Sonny Boy Williamson The Bluebird Recordings 1938. RCA 86796-2.

Sonny Boy Williamson: (Rice Miller) The Real Folk Blues. MCA/Chess 9272.

Jimmy Yancey Eternal Blues. Blues Encore CD 52031 AAD.

Various Instruments

Blue Boogie; Boogie Woogie, Stride And The Piano Blues. Blue Note 0777-7-99099-2-6.

Blue Guitar. Blue Note CDP 7-06581-2.

Harmonica Masters. Yazoo 2019.

Jazz Archives Electric Guitar: from The Pioneers to the Masters. 1935/1945

Jazz Archives 84.

Piano Blues (the essential). Classic Blues CBL 200003.

15 Piano Blues & Boogie Classics. Arhoolie CD 108.

Rags, Breakdowns, Stomps & Blues; Vintage Mandolin Music (1927–1946). Document DOCD 32-20-3.

The National Reso-Phonic Instrumental Project. Time & Strike T&S 7787.

Slide Crazy! Rykodisc RCD 10346.

Violin, Sing The Blues For Me: African American Fiddlers 1926–1949.

Old Hat CD 1002.

Social Protest and Commentary

Blues in the Mississippi Night. Rykodisc RCD 90155.
"Can't keep from crying" Topical Blues on the Death of President Kennedy. Testament TCD 5007.

J.B. Lenoir From Korea to Vietnam. Blues Encore CD 52017.

News and the Blues: Telling It Like It Is. Columbia/Legacy 46217.

Josh White The Remaining Titles 1941–1947. Document DOCD 1013. Note: Quite a few artists recorded occasional topical/protest songs.

Chicago: Early Electric Blues

Chicago Down Home Blues. Audio Book & Music Co. Ltd. ABMMCD 1064.

Memphis Minnie Early Rhythm & Blues 1949. Biograph BCD124 ADD.

Otis Rush 1956–1958 Cobra Recordings. Paula Records PCD 01.

Howlin' Wolf His Best. Chess/MC A CHD 9375.

Elmore Janes The Sky Is Crying: The History of Elmore James. Rhino R7-71190.

Jimmy Reed The Best of Jimmy Reed. Vee Jay 1039.

Little Walter His Best. Chess/MCA CHD 9384.

Muddy Waters His Best 1947–1955. Chess/MCA 9370CHD.

R&B and Soul

Bobby "Blue Bland" I Pity the Fool: The Duke Recordings Vol. 1. MCA MCAD-2-10665.

Charles Brown Driftin' Blues; the Best of Charles Brown. EMI E21Y-97989

Ruth Brown The Essentials. Atlantic R2 76162.

Ray Charles The Birth of Soul — The Complete Atlantic Rhythm & Blues

Recordings 1952–1959. Atlantic 3 92310-2.

The Chronological Little Miss Cornshucks 1947–1951. Classics 5059.

Pee Wee Crayton Things I Used To Do. Vanguard VMD 6566.

Arthur "Big Bo" Crudup Mean 'Ol Frisco. Charly CD BM 50.

Bo Diddley Bo Diddley: The Chess Box. MCA/Chess CHC2 = 19502.

Willie Dixon The Big Three Trio. Columbia CK46216.

Fats Domino My Blue Heaven: The Best of Fats Domino Vol. 1 EMI CDP 7-92808-2.

Aretha Franklin Queen of Soul. Rhino R2-71063.

Lowell Fulson Tramp/Soul. Flair V21Z-86300.

Al Green Let's Stay Together. The Right Stuff T21Y-27121.

Ivory Joe Hunter 16 of his Greatest Hits. King KCD 605.

The Best of Louis Jordan. MCA 76732-4-79-2.

Professor Longhair New Orleans Piano. Blues Originals, Vol. 2 Atlantic 7225-2.

Big Maybelle The Okeh Sessions. Epic EG 38453.

Percy Mayfield Poet of the Blues. Specialty SPCD 7001-2.

Little Milton Movin' to the Country. Malaco 7445.

Johnny Otis The Godfather of Rhythm & Blues & The R&B Caravan Vol. 2 1950–1952. EPM 160412.

Junior Parker/James Cotton/Pat Hare Mystery Train. Rounder CDSS 38.

The Classic Rhythm & Blues Collection 1955–1959. Time Life 9604-1 OPCD 3558.

Etta James Tell Mama. MCA 088 112 518-2.

Albert King Born Under a Bad Sign. Atlantic-Stax 7723.

B.B. King Live At The Regal. Mobile Fidelity Sound Labls UDCD 01-00548.

Freddie King Larger Than Life. Polydor 931 816-1.

Kings of Blues; B.B. King, Albert King, Freddie King, Pee Wee Crayton.

Fuel 2000 302 061 186 2, 3012 061 210-2.

Denise LaSalle Right Place/Right Time. Malaco 7417.

Lonnie Mack Strike Lightning. Alligator ALCD 9189.

Dan Penn, Do Right Man. Sire/Warner Bros. 9 45519-2.

Ann Peebles Fulltime Love. Bullseye Blues BBCD 9515.

Esther Phillips Little Esther Phillips: The Complete Savoy Recordings. Savoy Jazz SLJ 2258.

The R&B Year, Vol. 2s. Audio Book & Music Co. ABMMCD 1119.

Jimmy Rushing The Essential Jimmy Rushing. Vanguard VCD 65/66.

The Sun Legend Rhythm & Blues Vol. 1. EMI Plus 72435761162.

Johnnie Taylor Who's Makin; Love. Stax STCD 4115-2.

Koko Taylor Koko Taylor. Chess CHD 31271.

"Big Mama Thornton Hound Dog" The Peacock Recordings Peacock MCA- 10668

Big Joe Turner I've Been to Kansas City Vol. 1. Decca Jazz MCAD 42351

T-Bone Walker T-Bone Blues. Atlantic 8020-2

Junior Wells South Side Blues. Delmark DD 628

Dinah Washington, The Complete Dinah Washington on Mercury Vol. 1 (1946–1949). Mercury 3-832444-2.

Wild About That Thing: Ladies Sing the Blues. Delmark DX 913.

Big Joe Williams Blues Masters Storyville. STCD 8002.

Jimmy Witherspoon Baby, Baby, Baby. Original Blues Classics OBCCD 527.

Chicago: Classic Electric Blues

Allison, Luther Serious Blind Pig BP 2287.

Lonnie Brooks Bayou Lightnin' Alligator ALCd 4714.

R.L. Burnside Bad Luck City. Fat Possum FP 1001.

Chicago Blues Masters with Junior Wells, Otis Rush, Magic Sam and Koko Taylor and Many Others. Fuel 2000 302 061 138 2, 302 061 209-2.

Boppin' the Blues. Charly CPCD 8271.

Robert Cray, Strong Persuader. Hightone Records 830 568-2 M-1.

Jimmy Dawkins, All For Business. Delmark DE 634.

Buddy Guy Damn Right I've Got The Blues. Silvertone 1462-2.

Earl Hooker Two Bugs & A Roach. Arhoolie CD 324.

J.B. Hutto Sidewinder. Delmark DD636.

Living the Blues: Blues Legends. Time-Life Music MSD 35881.

Magic Sam, West Side Soul. Delmark DD 615.

Louis Myers, Sins. Black Top BT 1049.

Sam Myers, Tell My Story Movin'. Earwig 4920.

Robert Nighthawk, Live On Maxwell Street. Rounder CD 2022.

Son Seals Midnight Sun. Alligator ALCD 4708.

Second Time I Met The Blues: the Best of Chess Blues Vol. 2. Charly CD Red 12.

Hound Dog Taylor and the Houserockers. Alligator ALCD 4701.

White American and the British Blues Revivalists

Long John Baldry It Still Ain't Easy. Stony Plain STP 1163.

Marcia Ball Gatorhythms. Rounder 3101.

Lou Ann Barton Old Enough. Antone's ANT 0021.

Rory Block Tornado. Rounder CD 3140.

Roy Bookbinder Bookaroo. Rounder 3017.

Roy Buchanan Guitar In Fire: The Atlantic Sessions Rhino 71235.

Paul Butterfield's Better Days. Rhino R2 70877.

John Campbell One Believer. Elektra 961086-2.

Andy Cohen Oh Glory, How Happy I Am: The sacred songs of Rev. Gary Davis. Riverlark Music RL CD 102.

Joanna Connor Believe. It Blind Pig BP 3289.

music by Ry Cooder. Warner Brothers 9-45987-2.

Fleetwood Mac The Original Fleetwood Mac. Pair PCD-2-1208.

Foghat The Best of Foghat Vol. 1. Rhino 70088.

Mary Flower Blues Jubilee. Resounding Records RRCD 408.

Sue Foley Young Girl Blues. Antone's ANTCD 0019.

Anson Funderburgh Talk to You. Black Top 1001.

Rory Gallagher The London Muddy Waters Sessions. MCA/Chess 9298.

Paul Geremia Gamblin' Woman. Red House RHR 54.

John Hammond Best of John Hammond. Vanguard VCD 11/12.

Ernie Hawkins blues advice. Say 'Mo Music SM 002.

Koerner, Ray & Glover: Blues, Rags & Hollers. Red House Records RHR CD 76.

Sonny Landreth Blues Attack. Blues Unlimited BU 5012-2.

John Mayall Wake Up Call. Silvertone 01241-41518.

John Mayall and Eric Clapton (Bluesbreakers). Deram 800086-2.

Charlie Musselwhite In My Time. Alligator ALCD 4818.

Tracy Nelson In the Here and Now. Rounder 3123.

Kelly Jo Phelps Lead me on. Burnside Records BCD 0015-2.

Rod Piazza The Essential Collection. Hightone HCD 8041.

Duke Robillard You Got Me. Rounder 3100.

Judy Roderick Woman Blue. Vanguard VCD 79197.

Roy Rogers Chops Not Chaps. Blind Pig BP 74892.

Roomful of Blues Dressed Up to Get Messed Up. Varrick VR 018.

Mark Spoelstra Out Of My Hands. Origin Jazz Library OR 2001.

Angela Strehli Soul Shake. Antone's ANT 0006CD.

Ten Years After The Essential Ten Years After. Chrysalis G2-21857.

The Blues Project The Best of the Blues Project. Rhino R2-70165.

Dave Van Ronk Live At Sir George Williams University. Just A Memory JAM 9132-2.

Rock and Roll

Martin Scorsese Presents The Allman Brothers Band. The Island Def Jam Music Group B0000589-02.

The Animals The Best of the Animals. Abkco CD 4324.

Chuck Berry. Ultimate Legends ULT 40422.

The Best of Canned Heat. EMI ManhattanDIOX 2438 CDP 48377-2.

Eric Clapton Unplugged. Reprise 9 45024-2.

Cream Disraeli Gears. RSO 823 636-2.

Bill *Haley & The Comets.* Ultimate Legends ULT 40192.

Jimi Hendrix; His Greatest Hits. Legacy International CD 460.

Janis Joplin Greatest Hits. CBS 30322.

Joy Of Cooking American Originals. Capitol CDP 0777-7-99355-2-9.

Elvis Presley The Complete Sun Sessions. RCA 6414-2.

Bonnie Raitt Luck of the Draw. Capitol CDP 7-96111-2.

Martin Scorsese Presents Stevie Ray Vaughan Vulcan EK 94095.

Johnnie Winter Guitar Slinger. Alligator ALCD 4735.

Z.Z. Top Greatest Hits. Warner Bros. 9-26846-2.

Cajun, Zydeco, and Louisiana Swamp Rock

Cajun & Creole Music 1934–1937 Rounder 11661-1842-2.

Clifton Chenier frenchin' the boogie. Verve 519 724-2.

Guitar Slim Sufferin' Mind. Specialty SPCD 7007-2.

Slim Harpo The Best of Slim Harpo. Rhino R2-70169.

Lazy Lester I'm A Lover Not A Fighter. Ace CDCHD 518.

Louisiana Cajun French Music Vol. 2. Rounder CD 6002.

Sound of the Swamp the Best of Excello Records., Vol.1 Rhino 70896.

Zydeco: Vol. One The Early Years. Arhoolie CD 307.

The New Black Blues Artists

Eric Bibb & Needed Time Good Stuff. EarthBeat 75265.

Ben Harper The Will To Live. Virgin Records America 7243 B 45591-2-0.

Corey Harris Between Midnight and Day. Alligator AL 4837.

Ted Hawkins On the Boardwalk. Munich MRCD123.

Kenny Neal Big News From Baton Rouge! Alligator ALCd 4764.

Alvin Youngblood Hart Territory Hannibal HHCD 1431.

Martin Scorsese Presents Taj Mahal. Columbia/Legacy CK 89080.

Keb 'Mo slow down. Okeh.550 Music BK 69376.

Philadelphia Jerry Ricks Deep In The Well. Rooster Blues R2636.

Otis Taylor Respect The Dead. Northern Blues NBM 0009.

Young Guns

Note: These artists are under 30, and are marketed liked rock stars

Jonny Lang & The Big Bang Smokin' Red Ink WK 24252.

Kenny Wayne Shepherd Band Live On. Giant 9 24789-2.

Beyond Category

Mose Allison I Don't Worry About A Thing. Rhino/Atlantic R2-71417.

Teddy Bunn 1919–1940 Guitar Solos, Vocal Duets. RST JPCD 1509-2.

Clarence "Gatemouth" Brown The Original Peacock Recordings Rounder 2039.

Dirty Blues Allegro Corporation CRG 220113.

Snooks Eaglin Country Boy in New Orleans. Arhoolie CD 348

Sleepy John Estes the essential. Classic Blues CBL 200009.

John Lee Hooker Modern Recordings. Flair/Virgin Records 7243-8-39658-2-3.

Jake Leg Blues. Jass Records J-CD-642.

Lonnie Johnson Playing With The Strings. JSP CD502.

Lonnie Johnson Steppin' On The Blues. Columbia CK 46221.

Murray Porter 1492: Who Found Who?. First Nations Music Y2-10015.

Saffire-the Uppity Blues Women Alligator. ALCD 4779

Sonny Terry Whoopin'. Alligator. ALCD 4734.

Robert Pete Williams Vol.1 I'm Blue As A Man Can Be. Arhoolie CD 394.

INSTRUCTIONAL MATERIALS AND VIDEOS

Books

Acoustic Blues Guitar Essentials (1999) San Anselmo, CA., String Letter Publishing.

Ainslie, Scott and David Whitehill (1992) *Robert Johnson: At The Crossroads, The Authoritative Guitar Transcrriptions*. Milwaukee, Hal Leonard Publications.

Arakawa, Yochi (2003) *Blues Guitar Chords and Accompaniment*. Torrance, CA, Six Strings Music Publishing.

Blumenfeld, Aaron. (1988) *The Art of Blues and Barrelhouse Piano Improvisation*. San Leandro, CA, P/F Publishing Co.

Bowden, Dan. (1994) *Mance Lipscomb: Texas Blues Guitar Solos*. Pacific, MO, Mel Bay Publications, Inc.

Bowden, Dan (1996) *Fred McDowell: The Voice of Mississippi Blues Guitar*. Pacific, MO, Mel Bay Publications.

Brozman, Bob (1996) *Bottleneck Blues Guitar*. Miami, Belwin Mills.

Carlson, Lenny (1993) *The Great Blues Guitar of Lonnie Johnson; Down in The Alley*. Pacific, MO, Mel Bay Publications.

Chipkin, Kenn, Pete Sawchuk, and Josh Workman (1999) *The T-Bone Walker Collection* Milwaukee, Hal Leonard Corporation.

Ford, Robben (1992) *Robben Ford II: the Blues And Beyond*. Miami, CPP Publications

Glover, Tony. (1973) *Blues Harp*. New York, Oak Publications.

Glover, Tony. (1975) *Blues Harp Songbook*. New York, Oak Publications.

Grossman, Stefan (1994) *The Music of Blind Blake*. Miami, CPP Belwin

Grossman, Stefan (1992) *Blind Boy Fuller*. Miami, CPP Belwin

Grossman, Stefan (1993) *The Music of Mississippi John Hurt*. Miami, CPP Belwin

Grossman, Stefan. (1973) *Book of Guitar Tunings*. New York, Amsco.

Grossman, Stefan. (1992) *Mel Bay's Complete Country Blues Guitar Book*. Pacific, Mo, Mel Bay Publications

Grossman, Stefan. (1969) *Delta Blues Guitar*. New York, Oak.

Grossman, Stefan. (1970) *Ragtime Blues Guitarists*. New York, Oak.

Grossman, Stefan. (1974) *Rev. Gary Davis Blues Guitar*. New York, Oak.

Grossman, Stefan and Woody Mann (1993) *The Roots of Robert Johnson*. Pacific, MO, Mel Bay Publications

Grossman, Stefan. (1968) *The Country Blues Guitar*. New York, Oak.

Guitar One Approved. (2002) *Slide Guitar Classics*. New York, Cherry Lane Music

Heaps-Nelson, George and Barbara McClintock Koehler. (19760) *Folk and Blues Harmoiica; An Instruction Manual*. Pacific, Mo, Mel Bay Publications.

James, Steve. (1999) *Roots And Blues: Fingerstyle Guitar*. San Anselmo, String Letter Publications

Kriss, Eric. (1974) *Barrelhouse & Boogie Piano*. New York, Oak Publications.

Kriss, Eric. (1973) *Six Blues-Roots Pianists*. New York, Oak Publications.

Lewman, Harry. (1998) *Leadbelly: No Stranger to the Blues*. New York, TRO

Lieberman, Julie Lyon. (1986) *Folk Fiddle*. New York, Oak Publications.

Mann, Woody. (1993) *the Anthology of Blues Guitar*. New York, Oak Publications.

Mann, Woody. (1996) *Bottleneck Blues Guitar*. New York, Oak Publications.

Mann, Woody. (1973) *Six Black Blues Guitarists*. New York, Oak.

Mann, Woody. (2003) *The Art of Acoustic Blues Guitar: Ragtime and Gospel* New York, Oak Publications.

McGhee, Brownie and Happy Traum. (1971) *Blues Styles of Brownie McGhee*. New York, Oak Publications.

Morgan, Tommy. (1971) *Blues Harmonica*. Los Angeles, Gwyn Publications.

Newquist, H.P. and Rich Maloof. (2002) *The Blues-Rock Masters*. San Francisco, CA, Backbeat Books

No Author Listed. (1991) *I Gotta Right To Play The Blues*. Hasbrouck Heights, NJ, Pearl Music.

Perrin, Jeff, Transcriber. (undated) *The Skip James Blues Collection*. Milwaukee, Hal Leonard Corporation.

Roth, Arlen. (1975) *Traditional, Country and Electric Slide Guitar*. New York, Oak Publications

Reese, Hampton. (no date) *B.B. King Blues Guitar*. Milwaukee, Hal Leonard Corporation

Rubin, Dave. (no date) *Chicago Blues*. Milwaukee, Hal Loenard Corporation

Seeger, Pete and Julius Lester. (1965) *The 12 String Guitar As Played By Leadbelly*. New York, Oak.

Silverman, Jerry. (1964) *The Art of the Folk Blues Guitar*. New York, Oak.

Silverman, Jerry. (1976) *Ragtime Guitar*. New York, Chappell and Co.

Smith, Arvid Burman Jr. and Barbara McClintock Koehler. (1976) *Contemprary Slide Guitar; An Instruction Manual*. Pacific, Mo, Mel Bay Publications.

Sokolow, Fred. (1991) *Learn to Play Bottleneck Guitar*. Pacific, MO, Mel Bay Publications

Sultan, Kenny. (1995) *Blues Guitar Legends*. Anaheim Hills, CA, Centerstream Publications.

Traum, Happy. (1968) *The Blues Bag*. New York, Consolidated Music.

Audio and Visual Materials

There are many video instructional blues tapes available. Homespun tapes in Woodstock, New York, has instructional tapes available for guitar, piano, and other instruments. Some are by such teachers as Happy and Artie Traum, others are by such well-known musicians as Dr. John. Stefan Grossman has many instructional tapes by himself, and by such other artists as Woody Mann and Rory Block. There are also "Music Minus One" style play along CDs for various styles of blues guitar. Major mail order retailers, like Elderly Instruments (www.elderly.com) offer large listings of instructional videos and recordings.

Performance and Documentary Videos

Stefan Grossman's Vestapol has issued a number of videos that contain rare performances by such artists as Fred McDowell, Jesse

Fuller, Son House, etc. The entire Martin Scorsese made-for-TV film series of seven shows is available on Legacy DVD's. Les Blank has made a number of fine blues films about Lightnin' Hopkins, Mance Lipscomb, and others. Rounder has issued a series of videos made by Alan Lomax. As with recordings, there are a wealth of VHS and DVD items available on individual artists, or on documentary aspects of the blues.

Blues Story: Shout DVD 31226.

Hellhounds On My Trail: the Afterlife of Robert Johnson. Center Stage DVD WHE 73052.

Last of the Mississippi Jukes. Sanctuary DVD 06076 99345-9.

The Life and Music of Robert Johnson; Can't You Hear The Wind Howl? DVD Shout 30181.

The Search For Robert Johnson. DVD Sony 481 13.

INDEX